# Attention!

**Adweek Books** is designed to present interesting, insightful books for the general business reader and for professionals in the worlds of media, marketing, and advertising.

These are innovative, creative books that address the challenges and opportunities of these industries, written by leaders in the business. Some of our writers head their own companies, others have worked their way up to the top of their field in large multinationals. But they share a knowledge of their craft and a desire to enlighten others.

We hope readers will find these books as helpful and inspiring as *Adweek*, *Brandweek*, and *Mediaweek* magazines.

## Published

*Disruption: Overturning Conventions and Shaking Up the Marketplace,* Jean-Marie Dru

*Under the Radar: Talking to Today's Cynical Consumer,* Jonathan Bond and Richard Kirshenbaum

*Truth, Lies and Advertising: The Art of Account Planning,* Jon Steel

*Hey, Whipple, Squeeze This: A Guide to Creating Great Ads,* Luke Sullivan

*Eating the Big Fish: How Challenger Brands Can Compete Against Brand Leaders,* Adam Morgan

*Warp-Speed Branding: The Impact of Technology on Marketing,* Agnieszka Winkler

*Creative Company: How St. Luke's Became "the Ad Agency to End All Ad Agencies,"* Andy Law

*Another One Bites the Grass: Making Sense of International Advertising,* Simon Anholt

*Attention! How to Interrupt, Yell, Whisper and Touch Consumers,* Ken Sacharin

# Attention!

*How to Interrupt, Yell, Whisper,*
*and Touch Consumers*

## Ken Sacharin

## John Wiley & Sons, Inc.

New York • Chichester • Weinheim • Brisbane • Singapore • Toronto

ISBN 0-471-38997-8

To Miranda, Emily, and Miranda's Uncle Jerry

# Contents

# Preface

*When you come to a fork in the road, take it.*
*Lawrence Peter Berra (Yogi)*

This is a book about people's attention. How marketers can get it and how they can keep it. The book describes a new set of methods for gaining attention—a new *mechanics* for getting noticed. I call the approach *attention mechanics*.

This book is also a counterbalance to the "new" conventional wisdom in marketing circles—that customer loyalty is everything. Customer loyalty marketing comes in many guises—relationship marketing, one-to-one marketing, database marketing, customer relationship management, permission marketing—and all of these say something important. But the fact is, marketers can't build loyalty unless they can get attention first, and marketers can no longer take the consumer's attention for granted.

The time has come to pay attention . . . to attention.

The problem is, getting attention is no longer a simple matter. We're overwhelmed with the explosive growth in new media forms. We're confused by the rise of complex technologies whose standards change just as we have mastered the previous version. We're anxious about the frenzied pace of modern life. We can't keep up with the demand that we always be in touch, always on, always connected.

Ads are now everywhere—not just on TV, radio, billboards, and print, but in bathrooms, on luggage carousels, on bananas, and even on tattoos. The ongoing barrage of messages has deadened our senses. The constant noise is leading to an entire society with a form of attention deficit disorder. It's tougher than ever for new messages to break through our perceptual barriers.

Many marketers are responding to this situation in an obvious way—they're spending more to get the attention they used to take for granted. They're shouting louder. And when shouting stops working, they raise the stakes and start screaming. Short term, these ploys will work. But longer term, they merely exacerbate the problem.

This is the dilemma that attention mechanics attempts to solve—how to get attention without contributing to the problem of getting attention. Central to the solution is the notion that attention must be treated as a precious human commodity—analogous to clean air or pure water. If we expect attention tomorrow, we must preserve it today, even as we draw it down for our marketing efforts. In this sense, attention mechanics is the first "ecologically sensitive" approach to marketing communications.

The book is divided into three parts. Part I describes how and why the power of marketing is eroding. Part II introduces the central metaphor of the book—the crowded room. What does a stranger do to get and hold attention in a crowded room? Each of the stranger's actions becomes one technique of a new approach to planning marketing communications I call *attention mechanics*. Each technique has a separate chapter in Part II. Part III explains how to start putting attention mechanics to work for your brand.

This is a book for every marketer who spends more each year but gets less return on investment. This is a book for every advertiser and media professional who is concerned about the eroding power of marketing communications. This is a book for everyone who loves the advertising profession and wants to see it survive (and thrive) for another hundred years. And make no mistake, the survival of the advertising profession is in question.

Some would say that the advertising business is at the sort of crossroads that Woody Allen described in a fictional commencement address to graduating seniors:

> More than any other time in history, mankind faces a crossroads. One path leads to despair and utter hopelessness. The other to total extinction. Let us pray we have the wisdom to choose correctly.

To believe the visionaries, the advertising business is faced with a similar Hobson's choice. Not to put too fine a point on it, the pundits say that traditional ad agencies are dead.

We're dead because we can't adapt to new environments. We're dead because marketing communications are moving onto the Internet and eliminating the intermediary. We're dead because . . . well . . . we just don't get it! According to MIT Media Lab guru Nicholas Negroponte, any business with *agent* in its name is dead: ad agents, travel agents, talent agents. (At least we can count on companionship at graveside.)

Perhaps. But to paraphrase Samuel Clemens, rumors of our death are greatly exaggerated. And even if we are dead, so what? It takes more than death to scare us! Death is just another challenge for ad veterans to face. If we're dead, we're just one step closer to the possibility of reincarnation, if not redemption. If we're dead, we've got to change course. We need to move on. We've got to try something different.

On closer examination, the prognosis is not nearly so dire. We're not dead, but there is a problem. Ad budgets are not producing the results they used to. And it's not just advertising. The same is true for other marketing communications disciplines as well.

Direct marketing, public relations, sales promotion—even online banner advertising—are not producing the kinds of results they used to. And all of this is occurring while one of the world's greatest communications revolutions—the Internet—is changing everybody's ground rules.

To reverse the situation, we must rethink our own ground rules—all of the principles, techniques, tools, and systems that we've invented and refined over the past half century. Is TV really the most powerful medium to build brands? Do ad campaigns need effective reach to generate results? Does efficiency really equate to effectiveness? Our goal must be to find new approaches that are just as effective, if not more effective, than the ones they replace.

We have a saying at my ad agency: that our job is to build sales overnight and brands over time. This has always been our job, and it will never change. *How* we do it is the fundamental question we must answer. The question is the same, but the answers are different now.

This book is about new answers. It is based on new learning. We're learning that getting attention has become more important than getting persuasion. We're learning that effective branding relies more on how easily prospects can navigate your brand and less on glitzy production values.

An author once said that authors don't choose to write books. Rather, books choose their authors. That's how I feel about this book. The story of the growing importance of attention in marketing needed to be told. It chose me to tell it. It chose me because none of the current crop of other marketing books adequately describes the role of attention in the marketing process. It chose me because I'm tired of having to compete on the wrong things and of having to respond to agency search questionnaires that ask, "How will you make our media plan more efficient?" It chose me because, well, maybe it thought I had too much time on my hands. In that regard, it was mistaken.

I am Media Director of Young & Rubicam's Media Edge office in San Francisco. My job is to direct media placement across all media forms for our clients in San Francisco, including Sony, Chevron, and Adobe—about $250 million in annual billings. In my career, I have worked for a diverse set of clients in many different industries—Procter & Gamble, MGM Grand Casino, Novell, Sears Hardware, Hardee's restaurants, and British Airways, to name a few. I also teach advertising and media here in San Francisco. But my greatest qualification for writing the book is that I love this business.

Returning to the choice in the commencement address, if we have the wisdom to change, we can avoid extinction—and achieve utter despair. Actually, we can aim quite a bit higher.

May I have your attention please?

# Attention!

# Introduction

In an environment of unlimited selection and access to information, the scarce resource becomes customer attention.

*John Hagel III and Marc Singer,* Net Worth: Shaping Markets When Consumers Make the Rules

Several years ago, one of my clients gave us an unusual project. The client was a packaged-goods manufacturer, a classic marketer. The managers were worried. Something was wrong, but it was hard to pinpoint the precise problem. Every year, they increased their spending on advertising and sales promotion, yet every year they watched as the power of those investments declined. Every year their ads seemed as good as they had been the year before, perhaps even better, but despite that, the ads weren't producing the same sales results in the marketplace.

The problem wasn't confined to advertising, though. It seemed to be more widespread. In fact, just about everywhere they looked, their marketing investments weren't performing as well as they used to. Their coupon redemption rates were dropping. Their success rate with new product launches was off. It seemed that the best they could do was run harder and spend more each year just to stay in the same place.

The project they assigned us was this: Investigate advertising, public relations, sales promotion, direct marketing—all of the marketing communications disciplines. Find out what defines the state of the art today and tell us.

Ouch.

A team of us spent months on the project. We scoured the marketing literature. We talked to marketing professors at some of the top business schools in the country. We interviewed our own colleagues around the

1

world. We reviewed best practices for many of our largest global clients. And we talked to a marketing consultant or two.

All of these experts pointed us toward one conclusion: The state of the art in marketing communications today, they told us, revolves around how to engineer customer loyalty. Classic marketing techniques, such as those practiced by my client, were rooted in persuading and acquiring customers. But the new wave had shifted the focus from persuasion and customer acquisition to loyalty and customer retention.

Retaining customers and building relationships with them—through new techniques such as database marketing—was what the new game was all about. If we conceived of marketing as a building, then the bottom was persuasion and the top was loyalty. The company's problem was that it had to build its building taller. It had the persuasion bottom part completed, but it had barely begun to construct the top part—loyalty. Emphasis needed to shift there.

So, that's basically what we told our client. We had a nice meeting. Snacks were served. But something about that answer didn't seem to fit. It seemed to me that something obvious had been overlooked. It started an itch, and I'm finally getting around to scratching it—with this book.

Here's the question that itched: What's the foundation for this building? How solid is it? To build taller cannot be the first order of business if the foundation is not secure. An edifice on quicksand is not safe, no matter what the height.

The foundation for this building had to be *attention*. Marketers can't persuade people unless they have their attention first. Marketers can't earn customers' loyalty unless they have their attention first. Attention is the prerequisite for all marketing efforts. But in order to become a solid foundation for marketing communications today, attention needs some shoring up.

Persuasion-based marketing and loyalty-based marketing are two different, valid approaches. Attention-based marketing represents a third approach. This book tells its story.

In this book, I introduce a new discipline, *attention mechanics*, to help brand managers build a solid foundation for their marketing efforts. Attention mechanics is a reaction against the growing conventional view that persuasion-based marketing is dead, and loyalty-based marketing is the only discipline that can replace it.

Attention mechanics reconceptualizes the field of marketing communications around the notion of attention. It is an attempt to answer the question, "How can we publicize, advertise, and promote brands if we cannot assume that we have our customer's attention to begin with?"

Attention mechanics recognizes that marketers need both persuasion and loyalty. But putting the focus purely on persuasion or loyalty is a mistake for many brands. Attention mechanics represents a *third* way: neither persuasion nor loyalty but a synthesis of both. Attention mechanics offers new methods to guide the process of marketing communications planning.

# Part I: The Power of Marketing Is Eroding... from Lack of Attention

Part I describes the problem: Everywhere we look today, the power of marketing communications is eroding from lack of attention. According to one estimate, only a third of all ad campaigns have a significant impact on sales. Fewer than 25% have any long-term effect.[1]

Copy scores are declining, redemption rates are plummeting, and even online, banner ad click-through rates are dropping. In the past 30 years, our ability to recall TV ads has declined 70%, despite the ever increasing sophistication (and ever increasing expense) of TV production values. And the rate of deterioration is accelerating. It has taken only five years for click-through rates for web banner ads to plummet more than 90%. Recently, banner click-through rates have been dropping by almost a tenth of a percent every month.

In an attempt to recapture the previous power of Internet-based communications efforts, media planners are now gravitating toward e-mail as the new online holy grail. How long will it take for e-mail messages to lose most of their efficacy? Two years?

Most marketing communications can be synthesized into one basic strategy and two fundamental tactics: Influence behavior (the strategy) by maintaining or changing buying habits (the tactics). These are the basic tenets of almost all marketing efforts. Admittedly, maintaining or changing habits requires more than just attention. But if brands can't get attention, then nothing else is possible.

To borrow a metaphor from Darwinian theory, the attention environment is becoming inhospitable to ads. To survive, new, "fitter" species of ads are evolving. But the rate of advertising evolution cannot keep pace with the rate of deterioration in the attention ecology. As the attention environment turns inhospitable, ads must adapt to survive. One survival strategy is to specialize. Almost every day, we find reason to be amazed by new ad formats that exploit new niches. Ads appear on luggage carousels or on tattoos. On pagers and bananas. On cell phones and bathroom stall doors. "What will they think of next!" We are witnessing a "Cambrian explosion" of new ad life forms. But as rapidly as new ad forms evolve, their survival is undermined by even more rapid deterioration in the attention ecosystem.

The tendency is for successful new ad formats to overpopulate and overgraze their attention environments until, inevitably, they start to lose their attention-getting power. TV commercials have expanded to fill 20 to 30% of every program hour, while our ability to recall commercials continues to diminish. E-mail messages, once rare and welcome, have turned into spam. Online banner ads have multiplied to the point that they represent little more than annoying intrusions to web surfing.

The example of online banner ads is typical. In the mid-1990s online banner ads were intriguing novelties. We clicked on 10 out of every 100 we saw, just to see what was behind them. Today, banner ads (those gaudy, blinking neon signs of the Internet age) are omnipresent, but we now click on fewer than 1 in 200. Our attention spans have worn down.

The easiest and least thoughtful way to get attention back is simply to spend more, to shout louder. This is the path we've taken up till now. Shouting works fine until someone else shouts louder. When the whole market is shouting, only screaming will do. Mere shouting won't work anymore. That sort of escalation is driving and polluting the marketing environment today. We must find more creative and environmentally sound ways of attracting attention so that the power of marketing communications remains intact and effective for the future.

Here's another analogy: In much of the world, mortality rates have declined over the centuries. People are healthier and live longer now than ever in history. Why is this the case? The superficial answer is that advancements in medical science have contributed most to these positive outcomes: New drugs, surgical techniques, and medical technologies have improved our general health. Without question, these are part of the answer. But the deeper answer has to do with sanitation: cleaner water, less crowded living conditions, less pollution. The improvement in basic sanitation is a larger factor in the health of our populations than all of the advances in medical science combined.

To a marketer, attention is akin to the clean water and uncrowded conditions that lead to a healthy environment. To keep our brands healthy, we must carefully nurture attention before moving on to the more sophisticated concepts of persuasion and loyalty.

It's a paradox of life at the turn of the millennium: Information and choice are expanding exponentially, but our life spans remain finite. In such a world, attention is a scarce resource, a precious commodity. How we choose to allocate that resource has tremendous consequences for marketers.

Each of us has a fixed attention budget of approximately 20 to 30 million wakeful minutes to spend in a lifetime. Marketers should be covetous of that budget, because marketing cannot proceed without it. Attention is the spark that ignites the marketing process. Attention is a critical prelude to any marketing task. Persuasion, sales, and loyalty are the final aims of all marketing efforts, but none can be achieved without the consumer's attention.

## Part II: Getting Attention in a Crowded Room: The Techniques of Attention Mechanics

Part II introduces the solution to this problem: a new set of techniques, a new mechanics, for getting the consumer's attention. I call the approach *attention mechanics*.

Getting ads noticed is not a trivial matter. The "easy" ways—spending more to interrupt, shout, even scream—are wearing down. They pollute the attention ecology. They contribute to a vicious circle: Shouting starts to lose its edge, so marketers start yelling. When yelling stops working, marketers start screaming. At each step, the cost of entry rises, and return on marketing investment declines.

The overwhelming barrage of messages aimed at us every day has deadened our senses. As marketers, we must become more adept at getting attention. We need new methods to help our communications penetrate the psychological and technological barriers that our prospects are increasingly erecting. We have to get our ads noticed. Attention mechanics will help.

Attention mechanics is a new approach to marketing communications planning—the process of allocating the marketing budget and then designing and implementing programs across all marketing disciplines (including public relations, advertising, sales promotion, direct marketing, and corporate identity creation). Attention mechanics is based on the premise that we can no longer assume that we have our audience's attention when we attempt to communicate with them.

Attention mechanics is rooted in a metaphor of the crowded room. In a noisy, crowded room, the ploys a stranger might use to get attention point to the marketing strategies a brand could use to get attention in the crowded marketplace. These are the strategies that make up attention mechanics. Each chapter in Part II covers a different strategy on the attention mechanics ladder. The accompanying figure shows strategies that comprise attention mechanics. Attention mechanics starts with the premise that attention is a precious commodity that must not be squandered or abused. Shouting, screaming, and intruding get attention, but none is appropriate for attention mechanics. Attention mechanics starts with different, higher-order strategies—strategies that are sensitive to the preservation of the attention ecology. By presenting the strategies on a ladder, I do not mean to imply that marketers must progress through each rung to get to the next level. But I *do* mean to imply a hierarchy.

Lower-level strategies are less versatile—they're more likely to be effective solely to gain attention, but not necessarily to hold it. Higher-level strategies are more effective in both gaining and holding attention. Higher-level strategies are also more environmentally friendly—that is, they are superior at protecting and preserving the attention ecosystem. The *network* strategy anchors the top of the ladder, and this is the strat-

Strategies of attention mechanics.

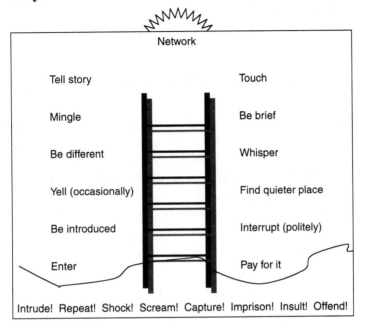

egy toward which marketers should most aspire. Every step on the ladder is preferable to the *intruding* and *screaming* strategies so frequently employed today.

Combined, the strategies of attention mechanics have two aims:

1. Restore the power of marketing communications.
2. Conserve that power for future generations.

We must adopt new techniques that accomplish our attention goals, but that do so in an environmentally friendly way, in a way that does not erode the delicate attention ecology, in a way that preserves the effectiveness of marketing communications. That's what attention mechanics aims to do. Attention mechanics is a mosaic of strategies and tools designed to gain attention in positive, restorative ways.

Attention is a most valuable human commodity. We must begin treating it as a natural resource to be conserved. We must find a more ecologically sound way of preserving our media and marketing ecosystem for the benefit of the next generations.

# Part III: Attention Mechanics: How to Get Started

Part III describes how marketers can begin to use attention mechanics. This part is focused on tools, applications, and measurement. I review all of the techniques of attention mechanics in this section and also propose new measurement methods. To ensure our marketing success in the future, attention must be measured.

Attention mechanics does not ignore the importance of more typical communications goals (e.g., goals based on a persuasion metric), but it does require a critical step back to basics so that our feet are on solid ground.

Attention mechanics aims to restore the balance among all the competing communications goals. Today, the balance is tipped too far toward the loyalty end of the scale. Attention mechanics compels marketers to place more emphasis (today there is little to none) on the *attention* end of the scale, as shown in the accompanying figure.

The premise of attention mechanics—that we can't assume attention—may strike some as trivial, if not odd. After all, haven't we always had to get people's attention first in order to sell them our products and services? Clearly, we have. But having conceded the obvious, we don't always act as if we understand the implications of this concession. Why?

One reason is that our advertising, direct marketing, public relations, and sales promotion "rules" are rooted in another time—a time not too

Balancing marketing communications goals.

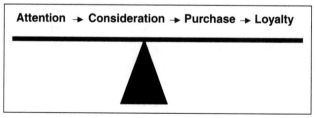

long ago when it was far safer to assume that we already had people's attention and that all we needed to do was inform, persuade, educate, and sell.

But conditions have changed. Marketing must penetrate a thick wall of ever present noise today. The quantity of information aimed at consumers is overwhelming them. To survive, they're blocking out messages—psychologically and technologically—to a greater degree than ever before. Marketers need to put more emphasis on getting attention. But we can't succumb to shouting. Paradoxically, we need to get attention in ways that don't contribute to the problem of getting attention. Attention mechanics can help.

# PART I

# The Power of Marketing Is Eroding . . . from Lack of *Attention*

# 1

# What's Wrong with Yesterday's Marketing?

As the immunity [to ad repetition] builds up, it costs more and more to advertise each year. It's like narcotics, it must be taken in ever-increasing doses to achieve the same effect.

Howard Gossage, cited in International Journal of Advertising, vol. 18, 1999

Traditionally, marketing communications rules have assumed that we had people's attention and all we needed to do was to persuade. For many years that was a valid assumption. But times have changed. Complexity is increasing in every part of our lives, and decision making has become burdensome.

Let's look at a few examples.[1]

## "Information, Please"

During an average trip to the supermarket each week, we spend about 20 minutes shopping. During that brief time, we have to sort through an average store's 35,000 items for the 18 (average shopping basket) we want to buy.

If we work in an office, we are inundated by messages—mail, express mail, e-mail, voice mail, pager messages, phone message slips, Post-it notes, phone calls, cellular calls. On average, we send or receive over 1,000 messages a week. Half of us report six or more interruptions an hour by online messages and other work-related communications.

Even when we get home, we're not insulated from the information blizzard. The average U.S. household sends or receives over 100 messages a week via telephone, mail, e-mail, pager, or fax. Eight of every ten of us are interrupted by an unwanted phone call at home every day, and 12% report receiving more than six. Most of us are spammed (i.e., receive unsolicited commercial e-mail) on a regular basis; over half of us receive unwanted e-mail messages every day, and some report receiving more than 10 unwanted e-mails a day.

Even when we're not checking our messages, we feel we should be. Over 30% of e-mail users are concerned that an important message might remain unattended if they don't check their e-mail frequently.

Our mailboxes are bulging with unwanted letters and solicitations. Advertising executive Peter Eder counted all of his home-delivered mail in 1998. He received 360 pounds of it, averaging 246 pieces a month.

Our technology is becoming increasingly complex. Microsoft Word included over 1,000 commands in the 1997 version—three times as many as the program had in 1992. (I know what 50 of them do, but I'm baffled by the rest.) Almost all of us would agree with Mark Twain's statement, "I'm all for progress, it's change I don't like."

Media are becoming ubiquitous, creeping into every nook of our lives, and we've seen explosive growth in media options. The average U.S. home can receive over 60 TV channels today, compared to just 7 in 1970. There are over 800 million documents posted on the web, and new web sites and magazines are launched every day.

Beyond traditional media forms, we've had new forms to deal with. Media technologies that barely existed 30 years ago (in many cases, hadn't even been invented) are now commonplace—first and foremost, the Internet, but also cable TV, satellite TV, VCRs, cell phones, remote controls, PCs, and so on.

We're bingeing on media. The average U.S. adult spends over 8 hours a day consuming media (10 hours if books, CDs, and VCRs are counted along with traditional broadcast and print media). This is about double the dose of our midcentury counterparts. Some of us have practically become addicted to rapid-fire media sensations. As with narcotics, we have to take it in increasing doses to achieve the same effect.

This proliferation in media is fragmenting audiences. When the media multiply, audiences divide. Audience levels are dropping for almost all traditional media forms. Broadcast TV ratings are down. And, despite the press to the contrary, cable TV ratings are beginning to erode as well.

Nonprogram clutter is increasing. The amount of time devoted to commercials and other TV program interruptions is at an all-time high. About 16 minutes of every prime-time hour are now devoted to interruptions rather than programming. This figure exceeds 20 minutes during some daytime shows.

Longer television commercial breaks are becoming more prevalent. Compared to the 1960s, commercial breaks are three to four times longer in duration.

Information density is increasing. The average news sound bite today is just 8 seconds, down from 42 seconds in the 1960s.

## The Data Dump

It's gotten to the point that media are being considered pollution. Information is piling up like garbage. David Shenk described it as "data smog." And the irony of our information age is that as we collectively try to rise above the noise, we end up creating more of it.

That has led the media to raise the volume with shock tactics: trash TV, hate radio, shock jocks, publicity stunts, sarcastic rhetoric, violence, and vulgar language. On one major TV network in the summer of 1999, you could watch a man pass a snake through his nostril and cough it up out of his mouth. That's showbiz, folks!

Some point to Hollywood as the culprit. In his insightful book, *Data Smog,* David Shenk blames the increasing vulgarity on information overabundance rather than on the media industry's lack of respect for the family.

Despite the ever expanding barrage of information, our comprehension of it is decreasing. "More and more, we will know less and less."[2] The gaps in our lives are filling up with media. We have fewer opportunities to stop and reflect. "Pauses are an essential part of human life, and we are squeezing them out," reflects James Gleick in his book, *Faster: The Acceleration of Just About Everything.*[3] He continues:

> The Sabbath was a pause, a crucial pause, for many humans . . . there was until recently a pause in stock trading at the end of the day. Now the world markets go all the time. There used to be a natural pause in the news cycle between the evening newspapers and the morning news. Now that is gone.

It seems that consumers are feeling out of control. Shoppers are overwhelmed and confused. According to recent Yankelovich Monitor surveys, 61% of shoppers are confused by all the sources of information available to them; 47% say having a large number of brands available for a given product confuses things and makes life more difficult; and 81% of employees feel a need to simplify their lives.

The more complicated life becomes, the more valuable simplicity becomes. Paradoxically, some consumers will pay a premium not to have to choose. In a wonderful essay for *Adweek* magazine, Debra Goldman explained why she was unwilling to switch electric utilities even when not switching meant paying a higher price:

> Non-choosers do earn a benefit from the extra money their sloth and disinterest costs—though it's not better service, a higher quality product or a more meaningful relationship with a brand. Dial tone is dial tone. Electric power is electric power. What we get is the freedom not to think about it.

There's an old saying that there are two kinds of marketing targets: those who will spend time to save money and those who will spend money to save time. We're witnessing a population explosion among the latter.

To survive, people's natural psychological defenses are taking over. Our brains are performing information triage as a survival mechanism. People are blocking reception and narrowing their focus. When we can't stand it anymore, we don't slow down, we shut down. We stop responding. We hang up. We delete e-mail messages unopened. We stop paying attention.

## Your Attention, Please

Psychologists have a name for this—they call it *attention deficit disorder*. All of us, to some degree, are succumbing to this information-age disease. We can see the signs in ourselves in these classic symptoms:

- We fail to give close attention to details.
- We make careless mistakes.
- We do not listen when spoken to directly.
- We do not follow through on instructions.
- We do not finish our chores.
- We have difficulty organizing tasks and activities.
- We avoid tasks that require sustained mental effort.
- We are easily distracted.
- We are forgetful.
- We fidget.
- We can't remain seated.
- We feel restless.
- We have difficulty doing things quietly.
- We act as if we're always on the go.
- We talk excessively.
- We blurt out answers before questions have been completed.
- We can't wait our turn.
- We interrupt others.

Our attention spans are collapsing and we feel oppressed by the clock. There's never enough time for anything. We're constantly running late. One-third of online shoppers will abandon a desired purchase if a web page takes longer than eight seconds to load. We look for convenience and time savings everywhere—even in our *One-Minute Bedtime Stories*.

We have reached our physical limits. We can't slice our attention spans any finer. We can't keep up with the pace of change. We are whip-sawed between distraction and boredom. Increasingly, we feel out of balance and out of control. Echoes Aleksandr Solzhenitsyn, "Our capacity for concentration . . . is being overwhelmed by a tidal wave of inordinate superficial information."[4]

Each of us yearns to achieve some sort of attention equilibrium in our lives. But balance always seems beyond our grasp. *New York Times* columnist William Safire advises us that we have a right to disengage:[5]

> [You] have a right to turn off. I say: Resist the 168 hour week. Buy unbugged cars and drive incommunicado. Trade during business hours. On vacation, vacate; on the Sabbath, sabb; on Memorial Day, remember. Treasure those out-of-touch moments. Become a member of the Great Unreached.

I have this vision of Safire madly juggling three or four tasks at once while rushing to finish this manifesto in time to meet his deadline.

When we do manage to disengage, when we're not feeling anxious and hyperactive, we're bored! We seesaw between two extremes—attention overload and boredom, media mania and media depression—with almost no pause in between. Over 20% of us claim to be regularly bored out of our minds. "This is perfect," reads the caption of a cartoon showing a couple lounging on the beach, "I could stay like this for the next five seconds."[6]

Our news media seize on particular stories—O.J., Monica, Diana—and propagate them into feeding frenzies. When we're not absorbed by the latest sensation, we withdraw—it's just a slow news day. If we are bored for too long, we become jaded and spoiled. Despite the fact that the average home has over 60 TV channels to choose from that provide over 1,000 hours of television programming each day, we complain, "There's nothin' on." Despite the fact that the entertainment industry increases its spending every year for top-notch writing, directing, and acting talent, we opine, "TV shows are a lot worse than they used to be."

It is as absurd as imagining Imelda Marcos opening her closet filled with 2,000 pairs of the most expensive shoes in the world and saying,

Ad recall is declining.

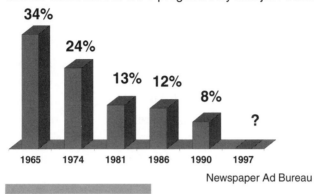

## Fewer people remember ads

Percent of adult viewers who could name one or more brands advertised in a TV program they had just watched:

34%

24%

13%  12%

8%

?

1965    1974    1981    1986    1990    1997

Newspaper Ad Bureau

"I've got *nothing* to wear!" (On second thought, she probably *did* say that a lot.)

We're paying less attention today, including less attention to ads. Fewer people remember ads. In a study conducted by the Newspaper Ad Bureau in 1965, 34% of adult TV viewers could name one or more brands advertised in a TV program they had just watched. The figure had declined to 8% by 1990—the last time the study was repeated. Almost certainly, the percentage today would be in the very low single digits, 3 or 4%.

Author Evan Schwartz has suggested that we are becoming the first society with attention deficit disorder.

## Technology Optimists

The optimists believe that technology will solve all of these problems. Remote controls make it easier for us to screen out TV commercials. And in the future, some argue, new technologies like agents and filters will shield us from messages we don't want to receive—which is going to make it even harder for marketers to get our attention.

Glenn Urban, former dean of the Sloan School of Management at MIT, could serve nicely as spokesperson for the technology optimists. In a recent interview with *American Demographics* magazine, Professor Urban explained his vision of a world in which virtual intelligence "advocates" will operate ceaselessly to advance your agenda.

Software agents and bots will roam the Internet hunting for deals tailor-made for you. They'll screen your e-mail and guard your computer's security. They'll remind you when it's time for your dentist appointment and set it up for you (hmmm, maybe this isn't such a good idea after all!). They will act as concierge and consigliere all rolled into one.

The optimists believe that the Internet is good, that it will connect us and deliver finally on the promise of McLuhan's global village. The pessimists see a dark lining in the silver cloud. They see the Net as a mixed blessing. Nets connect, but they also capture. If we're not careful, the Net will capture us, permanently tethering us to it. Today, being in touch 24-7 is almost expected. Tomorrow, choosing to be out of touch, at least occasionally, may become a necessity. We are becoming entwined by electronic communications. More than ever, we need to balance our connectedness with periods of quiet and anonymity.

Until now, new media technologies have been celebrated for giving us more choices and making information more abundant. But some observers are already challenging that notion. One-time director of the Freedom Forum of Columbia University, Eli Noam, observed that "the real issue for future technology is not production of information. Anybody can add information. The difficult question is how to reduce it."

## Fragmented Society

Another reason we're not getting attention is that we're not talking to some people, both literally and figuratively. *Literally* because there's a growing language barrier in our country, with 35 million Americans speaking a language other than English in their homes. That's more people than the entire population of Canada. But it's *figuratively* true as well, because the population in this country is becoming increasingly fragmented, which makes it more difficult to reach everyone with just two to three ads a year that offer two or three all-purpose persuasive claims and two or three generalized presentation styles.

In 1950, just 10% of the population was represented by ethnic minorities (black, Hispanic, Asian, Native American). In two years, it will be 28%.

Our task is especially tough given the major shift in attitudes we've seen. Only a few decades ago, people wanted to be perceived as part of the mainstream. Guilt and embarrassment were huge ad levers in the 1950s and 1960s, and advertisers did not hesitate to pull them. Typical was Cascade dishwashing detergent. Procter & Gamble promoted this brand by highlighting the shame a woman would feel if neighbors saw her dishes emerge from the dishwasher with water spots.

That was yesterday.

## Today

Today, the world is different. People are more likely to celebrate diversity and individual differences. Today, attention is no longer a given, and we need new approaches. Getting attention is an important new imperative.

There's a story about Albert Einstein that captures the marketer's dilemma perfectly. I can't verify whether it's true, although I've seen it written in several places, but it's a great story!

As a young man, Einstein was monitoring an exam for graduate physics students. Someone pointed out that there was a problem with the test he was handing out—the questions were the same as the previous year's test. Einstein is said to have replied, "That's okay, the answers are different this year."

And that's where we are, too. We have the same marketing questions, but the answers must be different today.

# Persuasion Physics

Over the past 50 years, a set of rules has evolved in the marketing communications industry to guide the efforts of practitioners. Some of these rules are based on empirical evidence derived from testing and experimentation. Some are rules of thumb—generally accepted beliefs and conventional wisdom.

Taken together, these rules form what I call *persuasion physics*. Persuasion physics starts by assuming we already have our audience's attention and all we need to do is persuade them.

Persuasion physics is largely a television-centric enterprise. Brand categories tend to have what I call *baked-in biases* when it comes to media selection. For decades, the baked-in bias (i.e., preferred medium) for most consumer household goods has been television. However, baked-in biases are not all the same. In the high-tech arena, the baked-in bias is print media, with a sprinkle of online seasoning. Persuasion physics and baked-in biases go hand in hand.

Persuasion physics places a premium on *impact, tonnage, efficiency,* and *effective frequency* (words and phrases that are a dead giveaway that a persuasion physicist is in the room). It treats communications as a series of discrete, carefully constructed, but mostly unconnected commercial units. Some say that the 30-second commercial is the most highly crafted piece of communication in the history of humankind.

Persuasion physics presumes that our job stops once we send this highly burnished, expertly crafted message into the marketplace. It expects that the medium's job is to deliver the message, period. Importantly, it does not anticipate a reply. (My colleague, Mike Samet, sometimes describes this belief as "media as mailman" in contrast to his views on using "media as lobbyist.")

Persuasion physics offers rigid rules for creating marketing messages. From David Ogilvy,[7] founder of Ogilvy & Mather, these are the steps for creating an effective TV ad:

- Open the first frame with a surprise.
- Use the name within the first 10 seconds.

- Show the package.
- Show the product in use.

And here are his tips for radio ads:

- Identify your brand early in the commercial.
- Identify it often.
- Promise the listener a benefit early in the commercial.
- Repeat it often.

Here are the not dissimilar rules for Procter & Gamble:[8]

- Plan to dominate—invest heavily to achieve leadership.
- Jump-start the commercial with a dramatic verbal statement of a problem ("My family wrote the book on stains!").
- Show the package in the first eight seconds.
- Demonstrate the benefit with a side-by-side competitive comparison or animated graphic.
- Show what you say, say what you show.
- Put the benefit in the visual.
- Connect the headline to the visual.
- Demonstrate the product in action.
- Wrap it up with a snappy tag line that mentions the brand ("Cascade. So clean it's virtually spotless!").

P&G's meetings with their agencies to review creative development are as rigid as their advertising rules. Here's an outline of a typical session:[9]

1. Brand Manager opens with a statement about the purpose of the meeting.
2. Assistant Brand Manager reviews the creative objective and strategy.
3. Account Executive describes how the creative development process was synchronized with the strategy.
4. Creative Director then presents the advertising.
5. Silent pause . . . for clients to finish writing notes.

6. Assistant Brand Manager responds first with an assessment of whether, and to what degree, the commercial followed the strategy.
7. Brand Manager follows by saying if he or she agrees or disagrees with the Assistant Brand Manager. ("I agree with Linda that the storyboard is on strategy. Overall, it clearly conveys that Zest is an effective deodorant soap, no matter what your age, and that it rinses away easily.")
8. The Brand Manager continues with remarks related to how well the commercial follows the "do's and don'ts" learned in P&G's Copy College.
9. The Brand Manager is encouraged to cite three or four positive things about the commercial. ("The way you describe how the man washes his armpit in the shower should be very effective. . . . The tone and interplay between the man and his wife in the opening of the commercial seems to be right on. It enables some tension in their dialogue as to whether or not Zest is the right choice, yet has an engaging charm.")
10. The Brand Manager might follow with three or four things that don't work or can be improved. ("I am a little concerned about *what* they are talking about in the opening . . . the double-entendre of the pregnancy test. . . . Double entendres in the opening have not generally been effective. I'm also concerned that the opening takes quite a bit of time. We don't get to the product until about fifteen seconds into the commercial.")
11. The Brand Manager summarizes with an overall assessment. ("I hope we can resolve these issues . . .")
12. The agency is allowed to respond.
13. The Brand Manager responds to the agency's response.
14. The agency responds again.
15. The Marketing Manager then . . .

You get the idea.

Admittedly, all of these rigors have earned P&G a well-deserved reputation for logical thinking and well-reasoned analysis. Unlike most competitors, P&G has been successful in extending these standards throughout its entire organization. Procter & Gamble is a prototypical persuasion physicist.

Whenever discussing hard-and-fast marketing rules, it is worth remembering the sage advice of Dr. Venkman (Bill Murray's character), the head mischief-maker in the movie *Ghostbusters*. After pursuing Sigourney Weaver's character throughout the movie, Dr. Venkman finally scores a date with her, only to discover, upon arriving at her door, that the demure violinist has been possessed and replaced by a sultry and seductive vamp. Sensing a good thing, Venkman decides to proceed with the date. He's no match for Weaver's character, however. She wrestles him onto her bed while he meekly resists with the protest that "I make it a rule never to get involved with possessed people." Undaunted, she violently embraces Venkman with a throat-scorching kiss. When he manages to come up for air, the dazzled Venkman admits his resolve has been broken. "It's more of a guideline than a rule." A helpful reminder for all would-be rule makers.

Although P&G's rules and regulations have been successful in the past, they may tend to stifle innovation in the future. And even if they don't, they may tend to slow things down—a side effect that could prove dangerous as the pace of marketing accelerates. If you practice persuasion physics, it's a risk that runs in the family.

Persuasion physicists believe in the concept of *effective reach*—the idea that communications effectiveness can be equated with frequency of ad exposure. Persuasion physicists believe in the concept of *efficiency*. Year after year they demand of their media planners, "Show us how you've improved efficiency!" Persuasion physicists believe in the concept of *targeting*—and their targets are often the size of small countries. They use words like *tonnage, impact,* and *target*. If marketing is war, then persuasion physicists are the field generals. They believe that if the weight of the message barrage is right and the creative is above average, then the brand will sell.

It would be tempting to suggest that persuasion physics ought to be discarded. But that would be too easy. Persuasion physics still works for many brands and situations. My view is that persuasion physics has been a valuable tool, but one that is wearing down. It still chugs along, but with continued wear it may soon stop working altogether. We need new approaches, not to completely replace our old ones just yet, but to expand the tool set we have available. Therefore, I am not advocating a wholesale abandonment of persuasion physics. The time is not yet right for that. But it *is* time to reexamine the conventional wisdom. It is time to *doubt*.

## Quantum Mechanics versus Newtonian Physics

Early in this century, some of history's most brilliant thinkers dared to doubt another entrenched model—the science of Newtonian physics. Newtonian physics was (and still is) fine for accurately predicting large-scale phenomena such as the movement of planets, the ballistics of a bullet, and so on. But it breaks down when applied to extremely small-scale phenomena such as the movement of electrons.

Einstein, Bohr, and others gave birth to a new physics: quantum mechanics. Its rules seem strange (for example, you cannot simultaneously know both the position and momentum of a subatomic particle—only one or the other). Yet its rules make accurate predictions possible in the subatomic world.

Over the decades, quantum mechanics has pointed scientists to new technologies that would not have been possible to conceive with a Newtonian mind-set—lasers, computer chips, supercolliders, and so on. Over that same time, engineers have continued to rely on Newtonian physics for other tasks—building bridges and going to the moon, to name just two.

Quantum mechanics has joined Newtonian physics to give scientists and engineers an expanded tool set. In the same way, *attention mechanics* adds new tools to our *persuasion physics* toolbox.

We need both disciplines to restore the effectiveness of marketing communications over time. That is not to say that persuasion physics and attention mechanics are interchangeable or equally applicable. They must be applied as conditions warrant. Increasingly, conditions will warrant attention mechanics.

Quantum mechanics focuses scientists on the most fundamental constituents of nature—subatomic particles. In the same way, attention mechanics will focus marketers on the most fundamental aspect of communications—attention. Quantum mechanics works in a world with a completely different scale—at the level of a single atom. In the same way, attention mechanics will work in a world with a completely different scale of communications noise.

# Push versus Pull

In the past, it was common to view brand marketing, especially in the packaged-goods arena, as a composite of two activities: *push activities*, which were aimed at getting the brand sold into the distribution channel, and *pull activities*, which were aimed at building demand among end consumers. A typical strategy was to push the product onto the trade's shelves with slotting fees and off-invoice allowances, then pull it through with advertising.

This push-pull dichotomy has been dusted off and reintroduced as a way to categorize marketing *communications* activities. In the modern parlance, *push communications* are old-style, intrusive communications. *Pull communications* are new-wave, requested communications.

Push communications interrupt the flow of an intentional viewing or hearing experience. Push messages are thieves, stealing our attention when we're not careful. By contrast, pull communications are messages that we *want* to receive. We willingly activate pull messages. We choose the time and the place to request them. We are in control.

In the black-or-white age we have manufactured, push messages are bad and pull messages are good. Push messages are intrusive and rude. Pull messages are invited guests. Push advertising is out of step with the times. Pull advertising is sexy and alluring.

Some argue that, in the future (specifically, because of the Internet), brands will no longer need push-type attention marketing. Instead, they argue, all marketing communications will evolve toward a pull model:

People will pull in the brand information they need when they need it. Agents, filters, and other devices will insulate people from noninvited messaging.

This view is directionally right, but wrong in its magnitude. There will always be a place for push marketing communications—unless, that is, manufacturers stop introducing new brands, existing brands stop announcing new features, and low-involvement brands (e.g., chewing gum, soft drinks) stop promoting themselves. For most products and services, push communications will continue to be the most important.

*Low-involvement* products and services are those for which the consumer perceives a low risk in choosing the "wrong" brand. These products and services are typically low-cost, impulse-purchase items. By contrast, *high-involvement* products (e.g., cars and appliances) entail a high risk for the purchaser who makes the wrong choice. Consumers invest a lot of time evaluating high-involvement product options. Even though low-involvement products and services may dabble with pull marketing (game-laden web sites, for example), they cannot survive without push marketing as the mainstay of the communications plan.

Here's an example of push marketing that won't die. Ticketmaster and CitySearch recently mined their online consumer profile databases for cross-marketing opportunities. And they found many. For example, they recently sent (pushed) e-mails to customers who purchased tickets to Bruce Springsteen concerts. The e-mails reviewed concert playlists and offered hyperlinks to purchase the relevant Springsteen albums.

Without question, we need to develop *both* skill sets—push and pull—to greater degrees of competency. But if forced to choose between the two, the astute marketer would do well to concentrate on the push side of the equation, where today more vexing challenges are arrayed than ever before.

If only black-or-white answers were required, then marketers could simply choose sides and accept the consequences. But in the real world of growing ambiguity, choosing black or white is not enough. We need a third alternative, a triangulation beyond the two well-worn positions: My attempt to offer marketers a more sophisticated approach is called *attention mechanics*, because attention is the catalyst for all marketing communications. Neither push nor pull would be possible without it.

# Before Attention Mechanics: Classic versus New-Wave Marketers

From the 1950s through the 1980s, persuasion physics came to dominate marketing theory. But in the past decade something new has happened. In just a few years, practitioners in the field of marketing communications have neatly divided into two camps. On one side are the old persuasion physicists, the *classic marketers*—a group anchored by packaged-goods traditionalists. On the other are the *new-wave marketers*—a group dominated by high-tech and dot-com radicals.

Classic marketers trained at our best business schools. They grew up in our finest companies—the companies that *invented* current marketing practice. In these hallowed institutions of capital, they learned the gospel of brand marketing, and they *believe*. From these holy lands, classic marketers spread out across the globe to preach the gospel.

Some characterize the classic gospel as *push marketing*—the idea that a marketing message can achieve its goal if it is intrusively pushed out to consumers with enough force and repetition.

Of course, as with any religion, there are variations. Some classic marketers are literalists. They believe that for every marketing situation there is an optimum formula for success. Success is all but assured, but only if they have faith in the formula and the grace to plug in the right figures (the right case rate, the right share of voice, the right persuasion score, the right efficiency, and so on).

Other classic marketers are "interpretationalists." They believe that the traditional marketing canon is metaphorically, though not necessarily literally, correct. Classic marketing experiences serve interpretationalists as guidelines to be applied with liberal dollops of judgment.

Whether literalists, or interpretationalists, classic marketers share a common belief in how marketing communications work. As mentioned earlier, I've coined the term *persuasion physics* to describe this concept. Persuasion physics is an engineer's approach to communications planning. Persuasion physics has served classic marketers long and well—especially when it comes to launching new packaged-goods brands. *Persuading* someone to switch from one fast-moving consumer-goods brand to *try* another brand is one of the greatest achievements to which a classic marketer can aspire.

And then there are the *new-wave marketers*. New-wave marketers don't believe the gospel of classic marketing. For new-wave marketers, the marketing god is dead. New-wave marketers don't act like classic marketers; they don't dress like classic marketers. They generally don't even *like* classic marketers.

New-wave marketers believe that the rules and principles of the classic marketers have calcified over time into an overly rigid and useless code. New-wave marketers believe that the old marketing rules are outmoded. They must be discarded or shed as a snake sheds its skin.

New-wave marketers see a world to which old rules don't apply. A world in which the internet is evolving beyond all previous communications channels. A world in which mass markets have shattered into microscopic tribes. A world in which people actively avoid mere ads.

New-wave marketers don't believe in push marketing. Their faith is instead rooted in the power of *pull marketing*. Pull marketing is the notion that people will pull in the brand information they need when they need it or, even if they don't need it, when they are properly incentivized to pull (i.e., offered some service in return or simply paid off). Push marketing can be resisted, avoided, tuned out, even technologically disabled (through bots, agents, and filters). Push marketing is ad pollution. Pull marketing, they believe, is ad conservation.

Classic marketers honed their skills mostly by succeeding at the *beginning* of the marketing process—by trial and by launching new brands. New-wave marketers focus their talents on the *end* of the marketing process—on loyalty. New-wave marketing yields not just sales, but loyal and committed customers, grateful fans, advocates, even evangelists.

If classic marketers are engineers, new-wave marketers are artists. To return to our religious metaphor, classic marketers are drawn to Genesis. But new-wave marketers leap right to Revelations.

Several new-wave visionaries have done much to expand our view of the role of marketing in the internet age. Seth Godin of Yahoo!, in his book *Permission Marketing*, has written convincingly of the loyalty-building power of pull-oriented, permission-based communications. (See Chapter 16 for more on Godin's concepts.) Don Peppers and Martha Rogers have reenergized the world of marketing communications with their series of books and lectures on the importance of one-to-one marketing and building loyal customer relationships. (For interested readers, I recommend that you start with their 1997 book, *The One-to-One Future: Building Relationships One Customer at a Time*.)

These new-wave revolutionaries have done much to enrich our view of marketing. They have focused a powerful microscope on what some classic marketers have simplistically dismissed as "repeat sales," and by doing so they have illuminated an entire new universe of possibilities.

Not surprisingly, the most visionary new-wave thinkers (e.g., Godin, Peppers, and Rogers) have attracted a rapidly growing throng of unquestioning devotees. In their rush to pile onto the new-wave relationship band wagon, some converts have trivialized the insights of the original authors, proclaiming the new-wave doctrine in terms of simplistic "about-isms":

"It's not about *persuasion*, it's about *permission!*"
"It's not about the *mass market*, it's about *one-to-one!*"
"It's not about *profits*, it's about *relationships!*"

When following the argument of some new-wave proselytes, one is overcome by the nagging sensation that marketing is a story whose plot we have completely misunderstood. ("About-sayers" are allied in a secret compact with "will-sayers"—prognosticators who proffer opinions about the future with rigid certainty, such as "e-commerce sales will overtake brick and mortar sales by 2007." A disproportionate number of about-sayers and will-sayers live in the San Francisco Bay Area and suffer, understandably, from gourmet coffee–induced dementia.)

## Attention Mechanics: The Third Way

The goal of marketing communications is to move prospects from attention to consideration to purchase and, finally, to loyalty (see the marketing balance diagram in the introduction). Persuasion-based marketing has long staked out the middle of that process—consideration and purchase. New-wavers have shifted the debate back toward the loyalty end of the spectrum. In contrast, attention mechanics restores the focus on *getting attention*, the spark that ignites the entire process. If classic, persuasion-based marketing represents the first way to market and new-wave, relationship-based marketing represents the second, then attention mechanics represents a new, third way to market.

As different as they are, classic and new-wave marketers generally share one common belief—that a prospect's attention is a *given*, a trifle not to waste time on, that the *really* important marketing activities have to do with what comes *after* (i.e., persuasion for classicists, relationships for revolutionaries). This is where attention mechanics parts company with both groups.

Attention mechanics demands a fundamental change in our mindset regarding how communications work. It is as if we are single-handedly attempting to shift the Very Large Array (the giant deep space dish radio antennas spread out over 27 square miles in the New Mexico desert). We are attempting to reorient the entire apparatus from a decades-long fixation on one part of the sky to a different, more primal region that we'd abandoned long ago as undeserving of scrutiny but that now promises to yield the most exciting secrets of the universe.

Attention mechanics aims to restore the effectiveness of marketing communications by refocusing our efforts on the most basic, the most primal communications' goal of all, the first and most fundamental thing a brand must do—*get attention*.

To be sure, attention is not the *only* thing a brand needs, but getting noticed has to be given a very high priority if we are serious about restoring the power of our brands' communications. What's more, we must get our brands noticed in ways that don't contribute to the problem of getting attention. Persuasion-based marketing or loyalty-based marketing won't do. We need a third approach. We need *attention mechanics*.

# 2

# What Marketers
# Need Today

Rule Number One is to pay attention. Rule Number Two might be:
Attention is a limited resource, so pay attention to where you pay
attention.

*Howard Rheingold*, Virtual Community

We need a solution today that will restore and preserve our marketing
and media ecosystems, one that will conserve one of our most precious commodities—human attention. To arrive at a solution, we start
by asking a common question in an uncommon way.

Typically, marketers ask, "What does our company need?" The possible answers are framed by the question. The answers in this case have to
do with market share, sales, profits, and so on. Typically, ad agencies ask
(especially those with account planning departments!), "What do consumers need?" The answers in this case have to do with product attributes, benefits, values, and so on.

But today, we start by asking a different question, "What do brands
need?" The answer to this question sets us on the path toward *attention
mechanics*.

Perhaps the most famous hierarchy of human needs is the one by
Abraham Maslow, one of the founders of humanistic psychology.
Maslow's hierarchy is often cited to explain certain universal needs people strive to fulfill (and in what order) in order to survive and achieve

Maslow's classic hierarchy of human needs.

satisfaction—both physically and psychologically. The hierarchy is also evoked to describe how motivations change within societies over time, as conditions, and thus needs, fluctuate.

Maslow's hierarchy is essentially a ladder, with the most basic survival needs at the bottom and the most aspirational, psychological needs at the top. The most fundamental human needs are physical—air, water, food, and sex.

Maslow believed that human growth is inhibited if needs go unfulfilled. People can't progress up the ladder without fulfilling needs on the previous step. Even someone dying of thirst would concede they would be far worse off if they were cut off from air, and so on.

It is instructive to think of brands as having an analogous hierarchy of needs. First and foremost, brands need *attention*—it is the air without which they will quickly die. But once they have it, they need understanding, affection, gratitude, love, and ultimately loyal relationships in order to grow and create brand offspring in the form of line and brand extensions.

Most conventional media advertising today works because of "borrowed" attention. The brand pays to borrow the attention of the audience to a program or editorial. Borrowing attention is inherently interruptive and often intrusive.

*Gratitude* is how most sponsorship marketing works. Gratitude is the emotion that most sponsorship marketing hopes to evoke and the basis

Brand's hierarchy of needs.

on which the relative success or failure of sponsorship dollars should be measured—but rarely is. Are prospects aware of your brand as a sponsor? If so, are they grateful? Do they express feelings of goodwill as a result?

Ironically, top-of-the-ladder needs (such as building loyal relationships) are becoming easier for brands to fulfill because of the ubiquitous Internet. On the other hand, fulfilling the most fundamental and basic needs, especially the need for attention, is becoming more difficult.

The explosive growth of media forms, the frenzied pace of modern life, the rise of complex technologies that cause confusion and anxiety are all contributing factors. Because attention has become so much harder to achieve, we must redouble our efforts to achieve it.

## The Content-Conduit-Consumer Spiral

Another reason that attention is uniquely important today has to do with historical cycles of business development. Every industry must produce goods (*content*), distribute goods (*conduit*), and sell them to a customer and cultivate his or her loyalty (*consumer*). To survive over time, a business must succeed in all three of these areas. Nonetheless, during any particular historical period within a business, one part or another of

The consumer-content-conduit spiral.

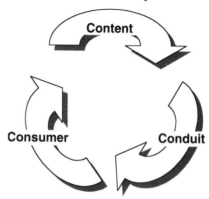

this three-way equation may predominate as the source of competitive advantage. Which part holds the key to success for a particular industry at any given time will vary, but over the long term, industries will cycle through periods in which the various phases advance and recede in importance. This endless spiral is shown in the accompanying figure.

Although the part of the spiral that is predominant at any moment in time varies for every industry and region of the world, understanding the historical direction of an industry's development is one key to understanding how best to compete. The following table shows some examples of industries and their spiral components.

| Industry | Content | Conduit | Consumer |
|---|---|---|---|
| High-tech hardware (business-to-business) | Hardware—assembled at manufacturing plant | Value-added resellers (VARs) | Business customers |
| Automobiles | Cars—built at the factory | Dealer | Buyer |
| Packaged goods | Products—manufactured at the factory | Supermarket | Consumer |
| Television | Programs—created by network/studio | TV stations | Viewer |

In the United States, it appears as if the conduit phase for many industries is now passing and a consumer phase is beginning. That is, it appears that the control lever in the buying process is changing from the channel to the consumer.

This is occurring at a time when Americans are celebrating their individualism and self-reliance. According to trend trackers such as Yankelovich Partners, two-thirds of us believe that the single most important change created by the Internet is the shifting of control from marketers to consumers. For better or worse, we are becoming more self-focused, if not more self-centered, than ever before.

We relish being in control. We want choices tailored just for us. We'll decide whether we're going to have a brand relationship or not, and we'll determine the terms: Are we willing to go beyond casual acquaintance to dating and marriage (not to mention trial separation and divorce)? We enjoy controlling our advertising consumption, and increasingly, we will equip ourselves with a vast array of information appliances to sift and filter the blizzard of messages aimed at us. We want to be in charge!

The marketing universe is responding to this "customer manifesto" by reorienting itself around the customer's gravitational pull, and U.S. businesses are rapidly deploying new "customer relationship management" strategies that organize their marketing and sales efforts around customer types. "These days," says Mark Shirman, vice president of customer management solutions at Cambridge Technology Partners, "companies don't compete on innovative products. Instead, the big differentiator is an innovative business model, such as the consumer-centric model espoused by Dell."[1]

In many sectors, the mentality of the *sellers market* used to prevail. Sellers were in control because consumers had few choices and little information about how to choose. Now the era of the *buyers market* is dawning: Consumers are bombarded with too many choices—at close-to-parity pricing. Consumers are learning that information about what to buy is readily available in many places—magazines, newspapers, radio, TV, and especially the Internet (cnet, epinions.com, productopia, deja.com, and so on).

Armed with information, consumers are taking charge of the marketplace. They're steering through the maze of choices and pricing. They have more power and more say than ever before. Consumers are learning that they can make the marketplace come to them by banding together in *demand-aggregation* clubs (such as Mercata.com and Accompany.com) to leverage the pricing advantages of group buying. ("My neighbors and I want to buy 500 pounds of paper clips . . . who's got the lowest price?") They can name their price for goods and services (Priceline.com). ("I'll pay $50 to fly from San Francisco to Los Angeles, but not a penny more!") They can even name the goods they desire and force sellers to haggle over who gets the order (Respond.com, iWant.com, eWanted.com). ("I want a 1965 cherry-red Mustang in showroom condition.")

It's apparent that brand managers can no longer control the marketplace and command attention as they once did. Consumers just don't have the time. Consumers want what they want when they want it. If we want their attention, we have to adapt.

As control passes from the channel to the consumer, the source of competitive advantage is also shifting—from superior distribution and penetration to superior attention and more receptive consumers. "Demand is in charge now, not supply," says Doc Searls, senior editor of the *Linux Journal*, "People on the demand side are not 'eyeballs' anymore. And they'll ignore you if you treat them like body parts."[2]

Consumers are taking control of the shopping and buying process for several reasons.

*First, there's more stuff to buy.* After a record economic expansion, consumers find few shortages of goods and services in any sector. In fact, typically they find the opposite—more choices than they know what to do with. When the economy is bountiful and producers must fight for share, consumers have an advantage.

*Second, they know more.* In the past, consumers couldn't easily find all the information they needed to make a purchase decision. A familiar brand name often swayed the buying decision. Choosing a familiar brand was easy when detailed knowledge was hard to come by. "Nobody ever got fired for buying IBM" was an old saying among risk-averse technology buyers in large companies. When buyers wanted to know more, they often had to rely on the intermediaries in the distribution chain—for example, the salesperson in the retail store or the value-added reseller.

In the current consumer era, attention is a competitive advantage.

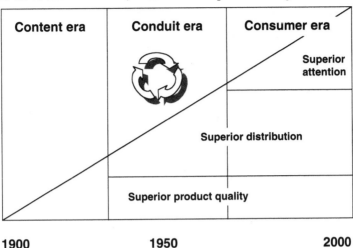

| Content era | Conduit era | Consumer era |
| --- | --- | --- |

Superior attention

Superior distribution

Superior product quality

**1900**  **1950**  **2000**

With the rise of the Internet, consumers are more knowledgeable about what to buy. They can directly access any information they need. They can comparison shop with ease. In this new environment, familiar brand names and salespeople are less important influences. Information that is highly relevant and customized often makes the difference now. Information gives consumers control.

*Third, technology makes it easy.* Computer and Internet technologies (search engines, bots, filters, customized portals, opt-in e-mail, and so on) enable consumers to gather all of this information, as a wave of new business models surges across the Internet—demand-aggregation systems (which combine consumers' buying power to secure volume discounts from manufacturers), reverse auctions (in which consumers post messages describing what they want and multiple sellers respond with bids), buying guides, and comparison-shopping engines.

According to Justin Hibbard, a reporter with *Red Herring* magazine, the new models "assume that consumers have unprecedented access to product information and a surfeit of merchandise to choose from. Under such conditions, consumers can play retailers against each other, demand low prices and expect exceptional service. This is consumer Nirvana."[3]

## New Business Models on the Internet

| Business Model | Examples | Description |
| --- | --- | --- |
| Auctions | eBay, Yahoo! | Bring buyers and sellers together in a fluid marketplace. |
| Name your price | Priceline, Expedia | Buyers offer a price. Sellers choose whether to accept the buyer's price. |
| Haggling | NexTag.com, HaggleZone.com, MakeUsAnOffer.com | Buyers name a price, then multiple sellers compete with counteroffers. |
| Demand-aggregation/groups | Accompany, Mercata | Pool consumers' buying power to secure volume discounts. |
| Reverse auctions | Respond.com, eWanted, Imandi | Consumers post messages listing what they want. Multiple sellers respond with offers. |
| Buying guide/product reviews | Epinions, Deja.com, Productopia, cnet | Consumers write product reviews, rate products, and share expertise. |
| Gift registries | WishClick, Della & James | Consumers list gifts they'd like to receive. Prospective gift givers consult the site to determine what to give and whether that gift has already been purchased by another gift giver. |
| Collaborative filtering/recommendation engines | Amazon.com, CDNow | Seller recommends a purchase that the consumer would probably like based on the consumer's previous choices and/or those of similar consumers. |

*Sources: The Industry Standard, Red Herring.*

As consumers gain leverage, marketers are changing how they differentiate their brands. They are pushing differentiation downstream—away from product-based attributes and features and toward consumer-based customization and service advantages.

Evan Hirsh and Steven Wheeler have examined this phenomenon in their book *The Rise & Fall of Product-Based Differentiation*.[4] "An ever more intimate knowledge of consumers increases the push toward non-product differentiation. Issues such as convenience, availability, purchase and ownership experiences, and after-sales service become increasingly important. This inevitably results in differentiation and power flowing downstream into the channels and to end customers."

As consumers increasingly take control of the shopping and buying process, marketers are responding by changing the "sell." John Hagel, a principal at McKinsey & Co., believes that marketers "are going to have to evolve from a vendor-centric brand proposition to a customer-centric proposition."[5] Hagel and his colleague Marc Singer predict the rise of customer-centric brands:

> In an environment where return on attention becomes the key measure of performance, a new kind of brand will emerge—a customer-centric brand. Customer-centric brands have two components—they assure the customer that the vendor knows and understands that individual customer better than anyone else does, and they promise the customer that the vendor can tailor products and services to meet that individual customer's needs better than anyone else can."[6]

Ford Motor Company is one believer. According to David Ropes, director of corporate advertising and integrated marketing, Ford's role is to be "a customer-driven designer of vehicles." "Branding on the internet," says Ropes, "has never been more important because of the ability of the consumer to be in control. Before, product was king. Now, consumers have complete freedom to go wherever they want to go and make their own informed decisions."

As the buying leverage has shifted from content to conduit and now to the consumer, the source of marketing leverage has also shifted. Marketers who are more adept at gaining and holding the consumer's atten-

## Marketing Advantage

| Content | Conduit | Consumer |
|---|---|---|
| Consideration and persuasion | Purchase and loyalty | Attention |

tion will have the advantage. Consideration, persuasion, purchase, and loyalty will always be important—but attention is the scarcest resource today. Without attention, none of the rest are possible.

For many industries, content was king from the 1940s through the 1960s. For television, TV networks and studios held sway. For cars, the factory was king. In the decades of the 1970s and 1980s, power shifted to the channel—to the TV stations or the dealers. Power started shifting again in the 1990s, this time to the viewer and the buyer.

Assuming that each phase in this repeating spiral lasts for 20 to 30 years, then the consumer phase that we are now entering will last through the mid-2010s to 2020s. In other words, we are entering a period in which getting attention will become the sweet spot for many marketing plans—perhaps for decades to come. Peter Georgescu, chairman and CEO of Young & Rubicam Inc., echoes the importance of the new focus on the consumer: "In this world of excess supply rather than excess demand, the consumer is more than ever the driving force."

PART II

# Getting Attention in a Crowded Room: The Techniques of Attention Mechanics

# 3

# Entering the Crowded Room

*Attention is the hard currency of cyberspace.*
Mandel and Van der Leun, Rules of the Net

To understand how attention mechanics works, imagine entering a crowded room—a giant, noisy, unruly millennial New Year's Eve party, say, in a city where you are alone and a stranger—and trying to get attention. The noise is deafening. There are hundreds of people milling about. Most are already clustered into tight convivial cliques. No one is waiting to say hello and welcome you. Instead, everyone else is already happily engaged in conversations.

This is not unlike the challenge faced by our brands as we send them off into the marketplace. In just one industry, consumer packaged goods, over 20,000 new items (that is, with unique universal product codes) are introduced in the United States every year. According to a 1997 study,[1] only 1,000 of these new stock-keeping units were truly new products.

Consumers are overwhelmed and time-constrained, barely able to keep up with their own concerns. When confronted with your new marketing message, most people "just don't care." At worst, they are actively hostile to new interruptions. The crowded room is the new reality of the marketplace.

There are a number of strategies we might employ to get attention in such a crowded room. Each of these strategies offers a metaphor for marketing communications. Taken together, all of the strategies form the outline of *attention mechanics*, which begins when brands enter the crowded room.

# Enter

Just entering the room is a step in the right direction.

According to psychologists, humans are designed to sense changes and differences and to screen out irrelevancies. Artificial intelligence researcher David Marr (cited in Steven Pinker's wonderful book, *How the Mind Works*) describes *vision* as a process that reduces the images of the external world into a useful description by filtering out the clutter of irrelevant information. Consciousness is engineered to ignore sameness and attend to differences.

Faced with the overwhelming volume of sensory input available in the environment, our brains filter out far more than they allow in. If they didn't, we couldn't survive. According to psychologists, only an estimated one-millionth of the information reaching our senses enters consciousness. Of necessity, our brains perform information triage.

Just by entering the room, we cause a slight disturbance in the sensory field. Something has changed in the room, and some people will inevitably look to see what. The act of entering will, by itself, draw some momentary glances from at least the people standing closest to the door.

# Momentum Marketing

This predisposition to attend to *differences* partially accounts for the relative success of messages that introduce new brands as well as new ad messages for existing brands.

A wide variety of test marketing and copy research touts the benefits of ads that (1) communicate "news," (2) convey new information, or (3) are new to the consumer (have not been seen before). In general, news

Campaign architecture.

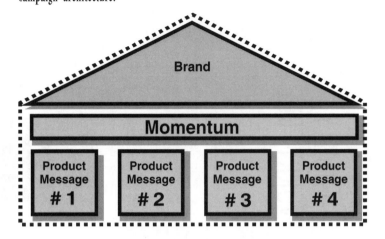

content and new ads outperform repeated or reminder ads. If a brand has news to convey or a new ad not seen before, it stands a better chance of getting attention.

Attention mechanics uses momentum marketing to exploit the power of news in brand campaigns. Traditional communications campaigns have one or two layers of messaging—typically a *brand image* layer, and a *product* layer. A campaign engineered according to the principles of attention mechanics inserts a third layer—*momentum*—into the campaign architecture between brand and product.[2]

Novell is an advertiser that understands the importance of momentum. For years the company battled the perception that Microsoft is the leader, or soon will be, in LAN/WAN networking software. The fact is, Novell is the clear leader in this arena, and a three-tiered ad campaign helps make the point that Novell is the world leader in networking software.

In one recent magazine campaign, Novell's brand ads communicated that Novell is the best tool for business because Novell's products operate across any platform—Unix, Microsoft NT, Apple, Netware, or Linux. With Novell there are no limits. By contrast, many other firms sell only closed-platform software products (i.e., products that will only work with other products on the same platform). Within the same campaign, Novell's product ads emphasized the unique features of individual

Novell's NDS product ad is Microsoft-friendly.

# FINALLY, WORRY-FREE NT.

Seems like everybody and his uncle is trying to install Windows® NT applications.

And when they do, a few surprises will be waiting for them. Because NT is a proprietary domain-based operating system.

So it doesn't integrate as seamlessly as promised. And it can require users to chuck their existing network investment.

But now you can deploy NT without having to deal with its idiosyncrasies.

You can turn it into an enterprise-capable open system supporting hundreds of third-party applications.

Manage access to and deployment of Microsoft® BackOffice™ applications such as Exchange™ and SQL Server.™

And lower the cost, complexity and redundancy of your entire network.

[ NDS™ for NT makes it possible. ]

NDS avoids the old-fashioned straight jacket of NT domains

by supporting heterogeneous environments of different platforms, different protocols, different people in different places.

NDS makes NT better. And one less thing to worry about.

Internet, intranet, extranet—anynet—the name of the net is Novell.

www.novell.com/NDS

## Novell.

Novell Directory Services

Courtesy of Novell. Reprinted with permission.

Novell's Southwest Airlines case demonstrates momentum.

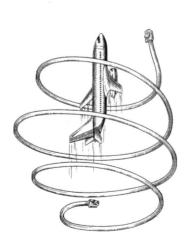

## HOW SOUTHWEST AIRLINES CONNECTED WITHOUT RESERVATIONS.

How do you get to be #1?

Southwest Airlines did it with on-time performance, baggage handling and overall customer satisfaction. Which made their business boom—and their network explode.

In 1991, Southwest had just 100 nodes and four different operating systems—and reservations ran on a separate mainframe.

None of these resources could communicate with each other, and administration was difficult.

Today, the airline has over 6,000 nodes running on just one operating system with seamless intercommunications throughout the entire system, all managed by just six network administrators.

Novell. NetWare. makes it possible.

NetWare technology is helping Southwest move into the future because it's the only networking software that can handle their rigorous requirements, such as putting 550 users on a single server.

Yet it has the stability, reliability and high availability demanded for a customer-dependent business.

And because NetWare is tightly integrated with Novell Directory Services™—the world's leading cross-platform directory service—Southwest can easily manage and control their entire network with single-source administration.

NetWare offers the best management and control of increasingly complex networks, including the Internet and corporate intranets, reducing overall network operating costs—and making all the right connections.

www.novell.com/netware

## Novell.
N E T W A R E

Courtesy of Novell. Reprinted with permission.

Novell software products, such as Novell Directory Services (the ad headlined "Finally, worry-free NT").

But the middle layer, the momentum tier, was arguably the most important element of the campaign. Momentum ads conveyed news about Novell's achievements and vision. The momentum messages telegraphed action, movement, and leadership. "How Southwest Airlines connected without reservations" tells the story of why a major airline just added Novell to their arsenal. In the technology world, where perceptions can change as fast as chips can compute, an ongoing momentum story is critical to success.

Of course, most brands promote news when it falls into their laps—when they have a new feature to tout, or an extension of the product to promote, or when a competitor slips up. Here's an example of the latter.

Several years ago, Motorola gave us an assignment to advertise its semiconductor "guarantee of a lifetime." But we had only a few weeks to do it—from project start to ads on the newsstand—because the Motorola ads had to run while competitor Intel's "floating-point controversy" still raged. Intel had recently introduced the Pentium chip, and a flaw had just been discovered in that chip—a floating-decimal-point bug that caused small inaccuracies to be introduced during some chip functions. Motorola wanted to emphasize that Motorola's legendary reliability is worth paying a bit more for. And it wanted to make that point while Intel was still mired in negative publicity. We met the deadline, and Motorola got the credit they deserve.

Seizing the opportunities as they arise is an excellent way to create momentum. Quaker Oats offers another example. When medical studies appeared promoting the benefits of a high-fiber diet, Quaker quickly produced an ad campaign to take advantage of that message.

If opportunities don't arise, then the attention mechanics manual suggests you create some. Don't just wait to react to infrequent or episodic news. Rather, attention mechanics suggests that marketers systematically plan and *manufacture* news—news about new features and extensions, of course, but also, news about important acquisitions, employees, sales, profits, what the CEO is up to, the architect for the new headquarters, and so on.

Echoes Michael Soriano Jr., marketing services director at Warner-Lambert:

> As brand builders, we must assure continuous development of new news, strive to be the first with the news and best consistent with how the news reinforces the brand's selling proposition. If we do these things, we can help assure that brands will enjoy long-term health and prosperity.[3]

# More Ads, Please

One clear implication is that we need more ads in our ad campaigns so that we can minimize repeat exposure and low-attention incidents. Conventional brand campaigns (those engineered according to traditional persuasion physics principles) tend to run fewer, but more expensive ads. For example, a quantity of three to five ads per medium is fairly typical for a single year. Some brands try to get by with just one or two ads a year. Brand campaigns engineered with attention mechanics will tend toward far larger ad pools.

Attention mechanics calls for ads that can be customized for smaller target groups and individualized for *window-of-relevancy* situations. Attention mechanics suggests that ads should be tracked and monitored far more closely than they are today for the slightest hint of performance fatigue—and retired if found wanting.

The cost per ad for an attention mechanics campaign should be less because we'll need to produce far more than we are accustomed to. My firm's experience with media planning for the web is instructive. Our rule of thumb is that brands advertising online must have a minimum of 40 executions per campaign.

For the online component of our clients' ad campaigns, it is not unusual for us to produce 50 to 70 different banner ads per quarter—a rate of 200 to 280 per year. Why do we produce so many? To promote relevance and protect against wearout. We tailor our ads' creative content to promote compatibility with adjacent online editorial matter. That makes each ad as relevant to the user as possible. Also, we need a large quantity of ads in our pool so that we can swap a fresh message for an existing ad at the earliest sign of click-through fatigue.

We are entering an era in which hundreds of database-enabled ads in a campaign will not be uncommon. According to *McKinsey Quarterly:*

> Today, it is acceptable to take three to six months to design one campaign and run it for up to two years. Tomorrow, a campaign of 300 one-on-one executions will have to be designed in two to three months and adapted continuously in response to real-time consumer feedback.[4]

Even today, the examples are plentiful. FasTV.com, a web site offering online video, can now select ads it shows viewers based on information extracted from massive consumer profile databases developed by Engage Technologies. DoubleClick envisions using its newly acquired Abacus database to serve up minivan banner ads only to people from households with three kids and a car that's more than five years old. From the *New York Times* to Charles Schwab, companies are assembling consumer profile databases to drive their online advertising efforts.

Indeed, attention mechanics points to a future in which ad messages will be "mass customized" by the thousands or maybe even by the millions. Ad messages will be personalized and tailored for real-time relevancy—and all of this will be enabled by powerful database technology.

## Grand Entrance

A leap beyond *entering* is *entering grandly*. A grand entrance exploits the actual moment of entry with as much noise, pageantry, and commotion as can be mustered to ensure attention. In a recent movie, Batman, cape fluttering around him, crashes through a glass ceiling several stories high into a fountain at the center of a party gathering, while his arch-nemesis pauses to admire the scene: "Now *that's* an entrance!"

Brands can make a grand entrance through similarly gaudy extravagances. The Windows 95 launch in August of that year was a case study

**Microsoft's launch of Windows 95 was one of the decade's premiere marketing events.**

Courtesy of Microsoft. Reprinted with permission.

Microsoft's launch of Windows 95. (Continued)

Courtesy of Microsoft. Reprinted with permission.

of a grand entrance. Many observers credit the launch of Microsoft's mid-1990s operating system upgrade as the first instance a software product crossed the high-tech/consumer goods divide to become a global general-consumer marketing success.

Microsoft assembled a huge arsenal of marketing communications to support the launch. Microsoft purchased the rights to use the Rolling Stones' "Start Me Up" as a product anthem. To preview the software to communities of technology specialists and editors who could influence sales, the company held giant meetings on launch day—with a million people worldwide.

Other launch tactics included Microsoft unfurling a 300-foot banner down the tallest building in Toronto, lighting the Empire State Building in Windows colors, hosting a party on a submarine (a world without windows), and sailing a four-story-high Windows 95 box into Sydney Harbor on a barge. Perhaps these were just the added-value elements for their promised schedule in *Sports Illustrated* magazine?

This was the greatest marketing moment in Microsoft's (and possibly consumer technology's) history to date. People lined up at stores so that they could be the first to buy the software when the stores opened—at 12:01 A.M.! All the fanfare proved successful, and Windows is now the dominant computer operating system worldwide.

Another way to make a grand entrance is to splurge—spend disproportionately to look your best and to make a big splash upon arrival. You do it by buying a new outfit, renting a limousine, and so on. Brands do it by splurging on their introductory advertising expenses.

For one of our clients, I recently compiled data on ad spending trends for 30 of the most successful new product launches dating from the early 1990s. Successful new launches were always accompanied by first-year spending blitzes. On average, first-year ad spending was two-thirds higher than maintenance-year spending. (*Maintenance years* were defined as the second year following the launch year and every subsequent year).

Heavy advertising support is most critical during a new brand's 8- to 12-week introduction period. Information Resources, Inc.'s *How Advertising Works* (analysis of approximately 400 Behaviorscan tests during the 1980s) indicated that new brands that spent most heavily during the introductory period were more successful than those that did not.

These companies spent millions each to make a "grand entrance" during the 2000 Super Bowl.

Courtesy of LastMinuteTravel.com. Used with permission.

This is the worst commercial on the Super Bowl.

But we don't know diddly about making ads.

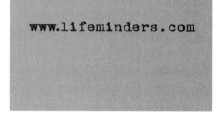

www.lifeminders.com

Courtesy of Pets.com. Reprinted with permission.

Courtesy of Lifeminders.com. Reprinted with permission.

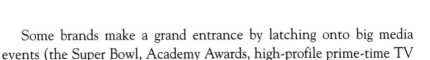

Some brands make a grand entrance by latching onto big media events (the Super Bowl, Academy Awards, high-profile prime-time TV shows)—CPMs be damned! Others do it by engineering novel, multimedia extravaganzas.

Take the example of Joe Boxer underwear. In 1994, Joe Boxer launched the world's largest e-mail forum on a giant billboard at the world's crossroads—Times Square. People could send e-mails for display on the board. The billboard was launched by Richard Branson and Joe Boxer founder Nick Graham, dressed, respectively, as Prince Charles and the queen of England. They were accompanied by 17 bagpipers in boxer shorts. Other tactics employed by Joe Boxer include sponsoring comedy shows with bus shelter ads featuring real underwear ("A show so funny you'll need new underwear"), rewarding showgoers with new pairs of Joe Boxers if they arrive dressed only in their underwear, and treating fashion critics to a transatlantic underwear fashion show on a chartered (Virgin Airways) jumbo jet.

Few brands can afford a grand entrance every year. But when a brand has news that can disturb the inertia of the marketplace, it deserves the splash that a grand entrance represents.

Wall Street has a saying: Buy on rumors, sell on news. Brands following an attention mechanics regime might spend behind rumors, but they always spend behind news.

# 4

# Interrupt Politely

All these ads claim my attention. This is fine if I happen to be shopping, but it was never my intention to shop 24 hours a day. I am giving away my attention, and my attention is all I've got.
*Adair Lara*, San Francisco Chronicle, *July 29, 1999*

After entering the room, you still have to connect to get attention. One tactic might be to interrupt: Walk up to the nearest person, stand close, and start talking.

This is a well-worn technique within the marketing world. It is the operating principle for most mass media advertising. Media buyers pay media owners to "borrow" some of the attention they attract, and the borrowing typically takes the form of program or editorial interruptions. Not all interruptions are the same however. Interruptions can be . . .

- Loud and in-your-face ("Hey you! That's right, you!! I'm screaming at *you!*). Crazy Eddie would find companionship in this group. His prices are "*insane*"!
- Offensive and insulting ("You're an idiot. Try to ignore me while I show off my tattoos!"). Or while I stand in front of the camera and belch every letter of the alphabet (ecampus.com).
- Captive and disrepectful ("Now that I've got you cornered, you'll *have* to listen to me! If you don't, I'll keep you imprisoned until you do"). One technique is the "trapdoor URL," which disables the Go Back command on your web browser. It works like this: When you land on an unscrupulous web site you dislike and try to execute the Go Back command, as many as 50 additional web sites appear.

- Outrageous and irrelevant ("We're the dot-com that kills worms!"). Or fries pet goldfish for dinner (ecampus.com). Or shoots gerbils from a cannon (outpost.com).
- Intrusive and rude ("Stop what you're doing and listen to me!"). Or EAT MORE BEEF, YOU BASTARDS—a billboard for the Australian Beef Council.
- Repetitive and annoying ("I guess you didn't hear me the first time, so I'll just have to keep repeating myself!"). This includes any car dealer's "Sale-a-thon" or that Pepsi commercial I don't like (each of us has one).
- *Polite* ("May I ask you a question?" or "Allow me to introduce myself . . .").

All of these techniques, except the last, rank among the least-imaginative ways to get attention. They work passably well—unless everyone else is doing the same thing at the same time. When confronted with this sort of marketplace stalemate, some brands continue to pursue, even to escalate, their negative attention-getting strategies. Novelist Rita Mae Brown once said that madness is doing the same thing over and over again but expecting a different result. According to that definition, some brands in today's marketplace would qualify for therapeutic treatment (or at least a leave of absence).

Even if a brand can gain attention by screaming or offending, it doesn't exactly put the brand's best foot forward to handle tasks higher up the communications ladder (informing, persuading, educating, and so on).

The best possible interruption is a *polite* interruption that is respectful of the needs of both the brand and the target audience. And the best possible polite interruption is polite *and* relevant at the same time.

## Polite Interruptions: Relevant Content Adjacencies

The most effective interruptions are those relevant to the conversation that's already under way. For the brand marketing side of the metaphor, that translates to interruptions that relate to the adjacent program or editorial. ("If you're interested in that, perhaps you'd also be interested

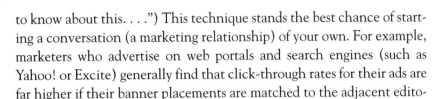

to know about this. . . .") This technique stands the best chance of starting a conversation (a marketing relationship) of your own. For example, marketers who advertise on web portals and search engines (such as Yahoo! or Excite) generally find that click-through rates for their ads are far higher if their banner placements are matched to the adjacent editorial matter and therefore relevant to the user.

Click-through rates for ad banners placed next to relevant topics are double the click-through rates for randomly inserted banners. Even more effective are banner ads that are engineered to appear as a result of a specific user search word or phrase (keyword-triggered ads). Keyword-triggered banners are clicked at three times the rate of randomly rotated ads.

The highest click-through response rate comes from *opt-in e-mail,* e-mail messages that the user has requested or has consented to receive. E-mail click rates can be 5 to 15 times higher than for conventional banner ads randomly inserted on web sites. Clearly, the higher the relevance, the more likely you are to capture attention.

For online advertisers, new techniques that sharpen our ability to deliver contextually relevant messages to prospects are now emerging:

*Dynamic messaging.* The ability to assemble the right message in real time from a database of possible message components and deliver it on the fly.
*Profile-driven inference engines.* The ability to infer a prospect's likely receptivity to a message by monitoring the profile of his or her histor-

Reported click-through rates.

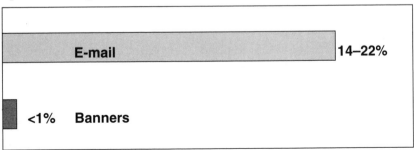

*Source:* Forrester.

ical clicking behavior. This allows advertisers to select and deliver the right message based on the profile.

In the offline world, advertisers are exploiting a growing variety of *ambient media*—previously ad-free locations that are all around us—to place relevant messages. AT&T arranges with hotel chains to imprint room key cards with information on AT&T dialing services. A local restaurant advertises on hotel elevator mirrors with the headline "YOU LOOK HUNGRY." A radio station encourages drivers to sample the station with a billboard ad that automatically displays the song the station is playing *right now*. Ambient advertising efforts can be effective, but only to the extent they provide relevant, just-in-time, and truly useful information to consumers.

Whether online or offline, highly relevant appeals can be effective means to attract attention. Interruptive advertising will continue to play an important role in brands' marketing plans. As long as the message is relevant *at that moment*, marketers can penetrate consumers' perceptual defense shields. A relevant interruption is not a rude intrusion, it's a welcome, useful piece of just-in-time information.

Several years ago, we used an innovative twist to create ads for Brita Water Filtration Systems that were considered welcome information rather than rude intrusions. We commissioned newspaper reps across the country to monitor editorials and stories about poor water quality in their local coverage area—stories that were sure to raise anxieties about the local water supply and thus serve as receptivity triggers for Brita advertising. As the daily reports rolled in, we reviewed them and made a go-no-go decision about whether to run a Brita ad in the appropriate newspaper, usually within a day or two of the original story date. We did not have a planned flowchart. The campaign was flexible, immediate, and powerfully motivating.

For Liquid-Plumr, we developed a "Clog Alert" program, placing ads on radio during peak drive time and on billboards near typically clogged (traffic jam) locations to draw attention to Liquid-Plumr's ability to eliminate clogs.

For Combat insecticides, we wanted to drive home the point that Combat continues to kill roaches even when you can't (you're away from home, you're home but in bed for the night, etc.). By pushing advertising off prime-time TV and onto outdoor boards, radio, and late-night television, we were emphasizing the solution to the relevant problem. If you're in the audience, then by definition you're not in a position to kill roaches . . . just imagine what the little critters could be up to in your absence!

Increasingly, marketers will view interruptive ads purely as door openers and discussion starters. Their purpose will be to attract initial attention and direct consumers to other communications channels where a dialogue may begin. The notion that marketers can use a single interruptive ad as a jack-of-all-trades will fade away. Interruptive ads can no longer carry the full burden of shepherding consumers along the path from awareness to consideration, purchase, and loyalty.

Remember, an interruption is just the initial contact. If consumers raise their hands, we will invite them deeper into our messaging system. In the world of attention mechanics, polite interruptions are just the start of something bigger.

## The Recency Approach

One aspect of relevance that is basking in scrutiny today is timing. It's easier to sell a snack to a hungry person than to one who's just finished dinner. It's easier to sell a mortgage loan to someone who's shopping for a house than to a person who just bought one. This focus on timing has produced a new media-scheduling discipline (tyranny?) called *recency*. Recency's most vocal proponent is Erwin Ephron, a convincing and elegant thinker and writer. In a nutshell, here is Ephron's recency argument:

- Ad potency is influenced by timing. The closer the ad is to the purchase, the greater the influence it will have.
- Reaching people many times is less important than reaching them at the right time.
- There is a psychological window of opportunity before each consumer's purchase.

- Advertising's role is to influence the brand purchased.
- Media's job is to put the message in the window.
- Since we don't know when that window will open for any given consumer, the most efficient strategy is to try to reach as many consumers with as few ad exposures as possible per week, over as many weeks as possible.

Says Ephron,

> From these many currents, the recency model reasons that 1) purchases are made each week, 2) close to purchase, fewer exposures are necessary, 3) but since we usually don't know who is ready to purchase, 4) the right strategy is to reach many target consumers, with fewer exposures and advertise for as many weeks as possible. It is skimming . . .[1]

Ephron's view is supported by a host of new studies on media scheduling, including John Philip Jones's analysis of packaged-goods brands' single-source data (add exposure and brand-purchase data collected from the same household), Walter Reichel's analyses of single versus multiple ad exposures, and the Adworks2 study by Media Marketing Assessment.

This bumper crop of scheduling insights is leading media planners to place renewed emphasis on timing and recency of ad exposures and less emphasis on frequency. As a result, in media plans all over the world today, reach stock is rising and frequency stock is declining.

Observes Ed Papazian, one of the country's most visionary media thinkers,

> What's amazing about the abrupt conversion from "effective frequency" to "recency" is how easily the former was vanquished. Faced with the recency theorists' "discovery" (that one exposure is enough), virtually every media strategist who, until then had blindly endorsed effective frequency, eagerly became members of the new media chic cult.[2]

Although recency should be a strong consideration in our communications planning, attention mechanics refuses to join the simplistic, bipolar, either-or debate: "What should my brand do—a recency-oriented drip-feed or a concentrated-frequency barrage?" The only right answer can be *both*. The *really* important question is *when?!* (See Chapter 7, "Yell Ocassionally.") Either-or is not acceptable.

For example, several years ago one of our clients, a retailer, asked us to help identify the optimum scheduling technique for its brand. Should the company flight its advertising? Should it concentrate on infrequent bursts? Should it follow the lead of the recency theorists and spread its advertising like butter, thinly but evenly across every week of the year?

To answer the question, we collected years of weekly tracking data— data on awareness, ad recall, attitudes, brand imagery, and sales. We tried out dozens of different scheduling variations in the marketplace, ranging from extreme concentration (a month's worth of advertising compressed into a few days) to extreme diffusion (advertising continuously but at extremely low spending levels). With the aid of computer modeling, we virtually explored thousands of other variations.

For this particular client, it turned out that neither concentrating nor diffusing was the best strategy. We discovered that the optimum way to advertise was not either-or, but both. The winning variation was a wavelike combination of two alternating methods—infrequent bursts of extremely concentrated TV advertising (which we dubbed *commercial flighting*), followed by low-level, but relatively continuous reminder messages in radio, outdoor, online, and community events (which we dubbed *bridge scheduling*).

Paleontologist Stephen Jay Gould's observations on wrong turns in the history of *his* science are germane to this discussion:

> I doubt that any rule enjoys wider application, or engenders greater trouble at the same time, than our propensity for ordering nature by making dichotomous divisions into two opposite groups.[3]

## Be Introduced

If you must interrupt, then the polite thing to do is to introduce yourself first. An even better tactic might be to arrange for someone else to introduce you, especially someone you know well. But the best introduction of all would come from someone special, someone whom others like and admire—*a celebrity!*

Implicit in an introduction is the audience's trust in the introducer. An introduction might imply endorsement: "I like this guy, so I'm introducing him to you. If he were a jerk, you wouldn't see me within a mile of the bozo. You might like him, too, so why don't you pay attention to what he has to say and see for yourself."

## Celebrity/Showcase Environments

In the past, brands that have used celebrity or organizational endorsers have hoped for just this sort of implied endorsement as a means to enhance persuasion. In the academic literature, this was known as the *source-credibility model*—the idea that the persuasiveness of an ad is directly related to the perceived expertise or trustworthiness of the source.

Brands that use celebrity endorsers hope that people will ascribe a higher degree of trust and importance to their brand by virtue of its association with the endorser. "If (so-and-so) introduces this product, it must be important, or (so-and-so) wouldn't go to the trouble."

Something similar is going on with brands that advertise in notoriously expensive media environments such as the Super Bowl and the Academy Awards. Brands are hoping audiences will credit them just by virtue of association with such expensive, visible events—and credit them doubly by dint of association with the other advertisers on the bill. "My brand is important! Look where I am, and look at all the other brands around me! If only Grandpa were alive to see!"

The source-credibility model has recently been criticized by some who view it as a weak persuasion strategy that rarely advances the brand's selling proposition. I agree with the critics. You can't rely on celebrity endorsers to do everything from getting attention to persuading to selling and servicing. In other words, they "don't do windows," but purely as attention-getters, celebrities are effective. In that narrow sense, they advance the cause of attention mechanics. Being introduced by a celebrity is an effective way to get attention, after which you can direct your prospect to other communications channels where you can talk at length about what's really special about your brand.

In attention mechanics, the role of celebrities is not persuasion but *attention*. In addition to the traditional persuasive advantage ascribed to celebrity spokespeople (the rub-off effect of an implied endorsement), attention mechanics recognizes the more immediate benefit: Celebrities are powerful attention getters. When brands need attention fast, celebrities can help them get it.

No brands in history needed attention faster than dot-com brands. Celebrity endorsers proved particulary effective for several. Cindy Crawford is spokesperson for Internet start-up eStyle, an online retailer for women. Although Crawford has received equity in the company in exchange for her services, her relationship with eStyle goes deeper. She sits on the company's board of directors. She recommends merchandise for them to carry. She conducts online chats with customers. And she has her own section of the company web site—Cindy's Corner.

*Star Trek's* William ("Captain Kirk") Shatner has performed the same role for Priceline.com, an online purchasing service. When it came to promoting the strange new world of online commerce, Shatner went where no celebrity had gone before—he agreed to be paid in stock options rather than cash. According to reports, Shatner's stock options in Priceline are now worth many millions.

Whether these celebrities will ultimately help these brands advance their core brand propositions is open to debate. But as attention getters they work.

Celebrities cannot be expected to shoulder the burden of the entire consideration cycle: persuading, informing, selling, and servicing. But viewed strictly as attention-snaring devices, celebrities work.

## Editorial Introductions

Many high-tech products and services have built their brands mainly (in some cases exclusively) on the introduction engineered by public relations. As in certain other fields (fashion leaps to mind), high-tech marketers crave the implied endorsement of their influencer communities—predominantly the editors and reporters who cover the industry in key business-to-business magazines and web sites. So introductions don't have to be made by celebrities or showcase venues. Introductions can come directly from the media in the form of editorial coverage. Favorable stories in the press are a form of endorsement—and can be a powerful introduction.

Its antitrust case notwithstanding, Microsoft has long been admired for the sophistication of its public relations. The company craves positive coverage from key technology reporters and editors and will spend what it takes to get it. In several instances, Microsoft has focused entire public relations teams on single reporters—scrutinizing every word they write and leaping at the chance to correct a "negative misperception" by offering to fly a team of Microsoft engineers to a reporter's office with proof of Microsoft's position.

Within media planning circles, there has been long-standing debate about the endorsement power inherent in the media vehicles that are chosen to carry ads. Some believe that the media function as mail carriers, merely delivering the advertiser's message, that the ad gets attention or persuades strictly on its own merits, and that media choices should be driven purely by cost-efficiency considerations. This belief is inherent in *persuasion physics*.

Others believe that the media can play a more important role, as *lobbyists* (this is my colleague Mike Samet's idea). That is, media vehicles can actively advance the advertiser's cause by imbuing ad messages with a halo of attributes drawn from the surrounding program or editorial matter. This belief is inherent in *attention mechanics*.

The power of various media formats, programs, or editorial environments to enhance or impede an ad's relevance has been largely unexplored to date. Most media research is aimed at identifying the size and demographic characteristics of the audience. As evidence mounts that timing and editorial adjacency matter, we can expect to see more studies of media environment rub-off effects, and these impact studies may someday prove more critical than audience "counting" for media planners.

# 5

# Pay for It

In the end, it may turn out that there's a cash market for human attention, the most coveted commodity of all.
*Thomas Weber*, The Wall Street Journal, *November 1, 1999*

There's one sure technique for getting attention in a crowded room—*pay for it*. As in many other endeavors, money talks. If all else fails, you can walk up to someone and offer that person cash to talk to you. This technique is straightforward and fair, an honest exchange—money for attention.

When I was writing this chapter, I couldn't keep the following image out of my mind, so you're stuck with it, too: In the movie *Mask*, Jim Carrey's character tries to enter a crowded nightclub but is rebuffed by the bouncer—rebuffed that is, until he reaches into both pockets, retrieves thousands of dollars worth of large-denomination bills, throws them into the air while coolly retorting, "You don't know me, but you may have met my friends . . . Ben, Grover, and Woodrow."

Ironically, the pay-for-it approach is the foundation for many traditional media business models as well. For example, TV and radio broadcasters provide (trade) free programming in exchange for attention. But fresh approaches are now emerging.

## Online Incentive Programs

In reality, exchanging money for attention is merely one version of the pay-for-it strategy. There are many others, and quite of few of them are turning into exciting new business models—online and off. Here are some companies that provide free Internet service in exchange for the customer's agreeing to accept ads:

- NetZero
- Freei
- Freewwweb
- Auric
- 1stup
- iweb
- FreeAccess
- FreeServe (United Kingdom)

NetZero, in particular, has experienced great success. Launched in October 1998, the company has already become one of the country's largest Internet service providers. Its model is simple: Consumers provide a bit of demographic information about themselves and agree to receive ads. In exchange, NetZero provides consumers with free Internet access—including web surfing and e-mail.

The central feature of NetZero's service is the ZeroPort™, a small rectangular window displayed on users' computer screens whenever they're online. The window shows a constant stream of ads. Users can move the window around, but they can't close it. This is an interruptive model of advertising exposure. But it is a fair exchange because NetZero provides value, in effect paying consumers to view ads.

The following companies offer cash, rebates, or redeemable points to customers who agree to accept ads and respond to surveys:

- Cybergold
- Netcentives
- Mypoints
- PointClick

Postage4free.com gives away free stamps and envelopes at its web site. The hook: The stamps and envelopes are imprinted with ads.

The ZeroPort™ streams ads in exchange for web access.

Courtesy of NetZero. Reprinted with permission.

Broadpoint Communications FreeWay offers free (ad-sponsored) long-distance service: two minutes of long-distance calling to anyone willing to listen to 15 seconds of advertising.

Free PC tested a service to provide a free personal computer and (initially) free Internet service if customers would agree to accept ads via an affiliated Internet service provider.

Many of these methods don't rely on cash per se but on the trade of information, entertainment, or service in exchange for attention. The pay-for-it approach runs the gamut from simple cash exchanges to rebates on product purchases to incentive systems to bartering attention for other goods and services.

Still, plain cash on the barrel gets plenty of attention. Frankenfield Associates Interactive couldn't get the desired response via telemarketing, so the company decided on money as a sure ploy to get people's attention, mailing $50 bills to prospects. (Don't expect to show up on the mailing list unless you can provide expert court testimony for personal injury lawyers. That's who Frankenfield is recruiting.)

A growing majority of pundits now subscribe to the pay-for-it approach as a successful method for marketing on the web. Information, entertainment, and service can be potent weapons to help a brand break through and get noticed in a world of shattered media choices.

# 6

# Be Brief

**A compression of time characterizes the life of the century now closing ... unoccupied time is vanishing.**
*James Gleick,* Faster: The Acceleration of Just about Everything, *1999*

Another way to get attention in a crowded room is to be *brief*. Say what you need to say simply and fast. Get in, get out, get gone. In a world of endless media choices, brevity and simplicity are more than virtues—they're becoming necessities.

In the brand's crowded room, it's all the more important to have a simple, focused selling proposition. And, it's all the more important to deliver that proposition concisely and consistently every time the brand has a contact opportunity—in every medium and communications discipline the brand employs, from packaging to media to personal selling.

## Hand-Raiser/Referral Messages

One reason we *can* be brief is that we no longer need to cram everything the brand has to say into every ad. Increasingly, brands will require a blend of different media forms to accomplish a variety of different tasks.

No single medium, and certainly no single ad, will be required to carry the full burden of all the brand's communications needs. Marketers will slice up the brand's story, and each ad will carry a piece of it. For

73

many marketers, this will represent significant change in how they have to think about their communications programs going forward.

Attention mechanics envisions a future in which many ads in a brand's campaign arsenal will exist purely to attract attention. These ads' main purpose will be to attract *hand-raisers*, people who have noticed the ad and express an interest in knowing more. Those who raise their hands will be able to dive deeper into the brand's story simply by following the indicated link or referral to some higher-bandwidth component of the campaign (e.g., the web). Each individual message will be merely one link in a chain.

This notion is liberating to the creative process. It is not critical that every ad message represent every conceivable copy point. In fact, that would be a mistake. Some ads exist purely to scoop up hand-raisers, and because of that (creative departments rejoice!) we can concentrate on making those ads *entertaining*.

One benefit of brief ads is that they're difficult to zap. The shorter the message, the harder it is to avoid. The best recent example of a short, zapproof ad was Fortune Brands' Master Lock TV campaign in 1998. To promote its well-known padlocks, Master Lock produced a one-second TV ad, just long enough to expose the company's signature image—a bullet striking, but not damaging, a lock.

## Scale Messages to Medium

Ironically, the Internet, a medium deeper than any ocean, is also driving brevity.

The Internet is developing along two paths simultaneously. The first is toward higher bandwidth and higher-speed access. New technologies (notably, cable modems and digital subscriber lines) are bringing higher bandwidth to more people. Higher bandwidth means faster downloading, richer images, deeper content, and more-compelling formats (such as video).

At the same time, the Internet is extending beyond its home base, the PC. It's seeping into every facet of our lives—our TV sets, our house-

The only one-second commercial ever produced.

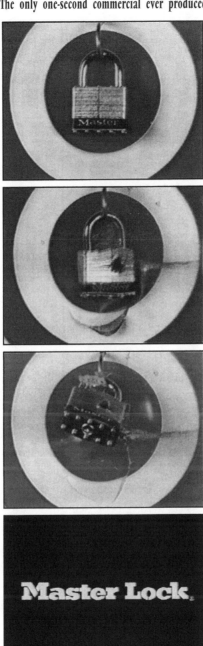

Courtesy of Master Lock. Reprinted with permission.

hold appliances, our telephones, our cars, and eventually, perhaps, even our clothes—much as electricity began to pervade our lives a century ago. Here's a sampling of new Internet-enabled gadgets:

- Motorola's i1000plus. Palm-sized handset that surfs the web and sends and receives e-mail.
- 3Com's Palm VII. The most popular handheld personal digital assistant (PDA) upgraded with web access.
- Research in Motion's Blackberry. A pager upgraded to send and receive e-mail.
- Qualcomm's pdQ Smartphone. Combines the functionality of a personal organizer such as the Palm Pilot, Internet access, ability to send and receive e-mail, and a wireless phone.
- NeoPoint's NewPoint1000. A wireless phone that can do double duty as a fax and a Palm Pilot–like personal organizer.

Many of our newly Internet-enabled appliances (pagers, personal digital assistants, wireless phones, and so on) don't have a great affinity for high-bandwidth messages. (I don't want, and will never expect, a deep message on my pager.) Thus, as the Internet expands its bandwidth in some devices, it will contract in others, and marketing messages will need to be scaled to the targeted device. PDA-targeted ads will be short and text-based, whereas PC-targeted ads may be long and deliver richer imagery. In a sense, this is merely an evolutionary step beyond current practice. Advertisers have long been accustomed to matching messages to media capabilities, pairing information-heavy long-text magazine ads with image-enhancing short-text TV spots, for example.

Even the physical elements of media technologies are shrinking. This point was driven home to me on a recent trip to San Francisco's airport. One of the concourses housed an exhibit of radios and microphones from the past 70 years. Early on, radios were built into large furniture cabinets, and microphones were enormous, ringed with the radio station's call sign. (Perhaps early media technologists wanted their inventions to look like *things* to reflect their sense of achievement.) Today, radios are tiny, and clip-on microphones are practically unnoticeable. With maturity, media technologies have blended into the background, becoming invisible, expected, and thought of only when they stop working. (At the end of marketing, one attribute remains to be promoted—reliability!)

Steve Kuhn, lead designer for Art Technology Group, predicts that when designers achieve the perfect interface for ubiquitous computing, it will not look like anything at all. It will shrink to invisibility. Tim Berners-Lee, creator of the World Wide Web, has observed that by 2020, it will be odd to say that we saw something interesting on the Internet, just as today it would be peculiar to say we saw an interesting article on a piece of paper. The Internet will fade into the background, as most previous successful technologies have done.

Paleontologist Stephen Jay Gould made a similar point several years ago in a study of size. He knew that animals and plants tend to get larger as they evolve (Cope's rule of phyletic size increase). But he suspected the opposite was true of—Hershey Bars! Gould studied the history of Hershey Bar sizes and found his suspicions confirmed—that is, Hershey Bars get *smaller* over time. From this he deduced the following premise:

> . . . that manufactured products of culture, as fundamentally unnatural, tend to follow life's course in reverse. If organic lineages obey Cope's rule and increase in size, then manufactured lineages have an equally strong propensity for decreasing in size.[1]

Media technologies, too, are "manufactured products of culture"—and they are getting smaller. Not just electronic devices, but magazines and newspapers have decreased in size over the decades. (I have a decades-old issue of *Better Homes and Gardens* that you could wrap around a Buick.)

Some marketers predict that the TV, telephone, and PC will converge into a single technology and that ultimately we will design marketing messages for one universal appliance. I believe this is a wrongheaded notion that drives a lot of silly debate over which appliance will win out—the PC or the TV. In my view, the TV, the PC, and the toaster won't merge into one device. Instead, the Internet will permeate a wide diversity of appliances, enhancing functionality as it does.

My colleagues at The Media Edge talk frequently about the need to hone our skills to "sell in a sound bite." I agree. Brevity is one of the building blocks of attention mechanics.

# 7

# Yell Occasionally

**We are becoming the first society with Attention Deficit Disorder.**
*Evan Schwartz,* Wired

Sometimes, in a crowded room, just entering and interrupting isn't enough. If the venue is particulary loud, you could still end up being ignored and standing alone by the cheese dip. All that money for a tux—wasted!

Under these circumstances, you may need to raise your voice to demand attention. You may need to *yell*. If you've ever been in a large, crowded auditorium prior to the start of an event, you've probably witnessed this technique: Someone gets up on the stage and says, "Everyone take your seats please, we need to get started"—and is ignored. Then, after pausing for a moment, the speaker cups her hands to her mouth and yells at the top of her lungs "May I have your attention please?!!!" The shock of a lone voice ringing out over the din quiets the crowd at once, allowing the speaker to resume talking in a normal voice now that she has commanded everyone's attention.

The secret to this technique is to yell only when you must, then resume speaking normally. If our meeting leader continued to scream even after the crowd had hushed, they would have considered her to be obnoxious, offensive, and maybe out of her mind.

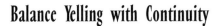

## Balance Yelling with Continuity

Brands in the marketplace must also yell, but they should resort to this technique sparingly and only when it really matters (e.g., they have important news to announce). Once they have captured attention, they should quickly dial down the volume and resume communicating normally. In other words, brands must yell—occasionally.

In Chapter 4, "Interrupt Politely," I described the case of a retailer who yells occasionally. With our strategy supported by a giant database of marketplace tracking data, we shifted this client's ad campaign to wavelike scheduling that alternates yelling (which we call *commercial flighting*) with talking normally (which we call *bridge scheduling*). Of the thousands of schedule variations examined, this pulsating wave of marketing communications delivers the strongest bang for the buck.

My colleague Austin McGhie often refers to the situation many brands face as "the inertia of the marketplace." He describes the process of brand management as "continuous discontinuity."

Over finite stretches of time, brand categories may appear to be stable, even stuck. Within its category of competitors, each brand's market share and relative position remain approximately the same, despite ongoing marketing efforts from most of the brands concerned.

It takes a lot of energy to disturb the inertia of the marketplace, shake things up, and change the order. But once the disturbance begins, the results can be dramatic. It's best if *your* brand is doing the disturbing.

## Yelling about Veggie Burgers

A bold example of occasional yelling is the recent case of Gardenburger. Gardenburger competes in the supermarket-distributed veggie burger category—a small brand in a small category, or rather, that was the case until 1998. In that year, tiny Gardenburger, with annual sales a mere $18 million, decided it was time to yell. The company decision makers boosted advertising to unprecedented (for them) levels. The centerpiece of their plan was a $1.4 million 30-second commercial in the final episode of *Seinfeld*—one of the most anticipated TV events of the year. It was occasional yelling taken to Hail Mary extremes. Nonetheless, it worked!

In one year, these were the results: Gardenburger sales skyrocketed from $18 million to $100 million. Its category share vaulted from 5% to 50%. Free publicity alone was worth more than the value of the *Seinfeld* spot—Gardenburger estimates that it received media coverage worth $2 million as a result of the ploy.

Marketing essentially reduces to changing and maintaining habits. Most of the time, the goal of advertising is to maintain habits. It does this by refreshing knowledge and restimulating interest in the brand's basic selling proposition.

It's easier to maintain an existing habit than to change one, but even that is far from a sure thing. It takes a consistent application of communications to keep the brand *interesting* and to keep it fixed in the customer's buying repertoire. Competitive brands frequently aim seductive appeals at your customers, and new brands occasionally emerge offering near copies of your brand's technology and service components. So, although maintaining brand habits may be easier than changing them, even maintaining them can be a formidable task. Without periodic reminders to maintain interest, brands can decline.

Coors beer is one example of a brand that has declined from lack of ongoing maintenance-level support. In 1985, Coors spent $43 million on advertising. Then Coors pulled back significantly. By 1993, the company was spending only $4 million annually for ads. From 1989 to 1993, Coors sales plummeted by 50%. "We've not marketed Coors as aggresively as we should have in the past ten to fifteen years," one Coors marketer admits.[1]

Without question, it's far harder to get consumers to change their habits and switch to your product or service. To do that, a brand must do something dramatic. To change habits, a brand has to shake things up. It has to disturb the inertia of the marketplace. Martin Oxley, with the marketing research firm, IPSOS-RSL, suggests that brands evolve through "punctuated equilibrium":

> The gradualist view of evolution would use a rolling ball metaphor: it changes smoothly and continuously over time. A more useful metaphor, however, is a polyhedron which can roll rapidly over from face to face, but resists change when it is sitting on one of its stable faces. Change occurs only when the threshold necessary to tip it over has been

Gardenburger's Hail Mary strategy put veggie burgers on the map.

Burgers 2

Garden 2

Hula 2

Record Player 2

Courtesy of Gardenburger. Reprinted with permission.

exceeded, and then the polyhedron will resist further change until that threshold is reached again. Between the [long] stable states, however, the transitions are very rapid. Punctuated equilibrium gives a much more accurate description of the dynamic nature of marketing.[2]

Some observers believe that the Coca-Cola Company has suffered in the past two years because it has focused too much on maintenance-level marketing and not enough on occasional yelling. Between 1997 and 2000, Coke's profits and return on equity have declined, and its stock price has significantly lagged the S&P 500 average. One recently departed (from Coca-Cola) marketing executive cited as a possible cause the neglect of any big stunts, high-profile ads, or glitzy marketing campaigns in favor of overreliance on maintenance-mode marketing.[3] According to the same executive, packaged-goods need an advertising boost every three to five years to inject renewed excitement into a brand. Instead, in the late 1990s, Coke's management focused market-ing exclusively on hitting the sure single rather than the ocassional home run.

Company marketers were forced into a conservative rut because of pressure from upper management to document the return on investment of every dollar spent on marketing. It's human nature: When you're under the gun to prove that everything you do will work, you must avoid risk at all costs. (The biggest news Coke made on the marketing front during the period was its decision to raise prices on its concentrate.) Coke is a brand that needs to yell occasionally.

Some disturbances are so severe that they can alter the complexion of their industries completely—even put large firms out of business. Pro-fessor Clayton Christensen of Harvard Business School has studied these phenomena and has labeled the catalysts of severe change "disruptive innovations."[4] According to Christensen, industries tend to be relatively stable until a disruptive innovation is introduced. Once that happens, the category disintegrates and the market fragments into specialty firms, which then emerge to dominate it. For example, decades ago, IBM dom-inated the computer industry. When PCs were introduced as a disruptive innovation, the market splintered and new companies (e.g., Microsoft and Intel) emerged to dominate the changed landscape.

Retailing has undergone four major disruptions in the past hundred years. First, railroads made giant department stores possible. Second, rural-free mail delivery led to mail-order catalogs. Third, the automobile allowed the creation of discount department stores on less expensive real estate at the edges of towns. And today, the Internet is completely eliminating distance as a factor and allowing new kinds of retailers, such as Amazon.com, to emerge.

Christensen's advice for survival is that a company must seize the innovation for itself and initiate the disruption, executing a bold company-changing maneuver with intuition and guts.

Over the long term, managing a brand means managing the alternating sequences of continuity and disturbance (or discontinuity). Brands must lock in a competitive position with a differentiated brand proposition and then plan periodic discontinuities—disruptive events—to stay on top. In terms of attention mechanics, brands must yell occasionally.

Professor Alan Middleton of York University in Toronto corroborates that balancing yelling with maintenance is the most important aspect of effective brand management:

> The key to successful branding is the balancing act between the need for improvement and the need for continuity. This ability to balance is one of the major challenges in marketing in the next decade or two—newness and familiarity, excitement and reassurance; these are no longer opposites but values to be balanced in every aspect of our lives and particularly in our purchasing habits.[5]

Yelling occasionally does not mean meaningless shocking. Even shocks should advance the brand's core selling proposition. Shocking merely to get your name out there is never an effective communications strategy. This is a lesson that many dot-com brands have learned the hard way. One example is CNET:

> Until very recently, shock tactics were a CNET staple. It raised eyebrows with an ad depicting a proctologist putting on a glove while his patient lay on an examining table asking for technology advice. "But

proctologists didn't fully explain what CNET is," Annie Williams, CNET's Vice-President of Marketing, explained, "we were always getting e-mails and hearing from people who all saw the ads but didn't know what CNET did.[6]

Yelling occasionally means turning up the volume. In brand marketing (even if a brand is doing it for a limited time) turning up the volume almost always requires more spending for more media. How can brands afford this? The same way our party guest prepares to squeeze into the tux . . . by dieting beforehand so he can splurge at the party.

Yelling occasionally requires the management of marketing funds over the long term such that maintenance/continuity cycles receive reduced maintenance-level spending to reserve monies for the yelling to be done later. Maintaining existing habits should cost less than yelling because it's the easier task. Change and disruption cost more to effect.

Metering marketing funds in this way requires a flexibility that the rigid annual ritual of media planning cannot deliver. Strict adherence to a yearly plan is not just boring, it could be dangerous to a brand's survival. Ad industry columnist Randall Rothenberg observes that "marketers need to be able to blitz their way to a boffo, Spielberg-style opening weekend—as Gillette did with its Mach3 razor—and also use the kind of canny stealth marketing that downtown nightclubs deploy to get themselves noticed."

## Flexible Planning: Ongoing Feedback and Adjustments

When (and how long) to yell and when (and how long) to talk are normally questions that can be answered only in reference to the natural rate of change in a particular brand's industry. For laundry detergents, a five- or ten-year planning horizon might be plausible. For Internet firms, a three-month quarter could be the planning limit (a year is forever and a decade beyond imagining). On the Internet, the cycle of discontinuities might have to be measured in weeks.

A continuous loop of real-time, input/feedback communications planning is common for state-of-the-art political campaigns, and it's not a bad model for attention mechanics, which requires that planning horizons remain flexible (i.e., not fixed to conventional time frames) and scaled to the rate of change.

# 8

# Whisper

> The real issue for future technology is not production of information. Anybody can add information. The difficult question is how to reduce it.
>
> *Eli Noam, Freedom Forum, Columbia University*

Sometimes, the best way to get attention is to go against the grain. Don't do what everyone else is doing—do what they're *not* doing. For example, a contrarian strategy for getting attention in a crowded room is to whisper—precisely the opposite of what your first inclination would be. Surprisingly, it can work, and when it works at all, it tends to work extremely well.

## Minimalist Content

Whispering strategies are appearing more frequently today. One example is the growing popularity of black and white (over color) in the media—from avant-garde fashion ads to music videos (*Love Is Strong* by the Rolling Stones) to art photography to TV shows (the hip, retro offerings on *Nick at Nite*) to outdoor billboards to films (*Raging Bull, Schindler's List*).

*New York Times* reporter Rick Lyman recently surveyed the growing popularity of black-and-white imagery in modern cultural artifacts. He calls it *visual whispering*: "Black and white in the midst of loud flashes of color is a sort of visual whispering. It coyly calls attention to itself."

DSL Internet access provider COVAD whispers by leaving most of the newspaper space unused.

Remember back in high school when "fast and easy" was considered an insult?

High-speed Internet access that's always on. Find out more at www.covad.com or call 1-800-GO-COVAD.

CO:VAD

The Internet as it should be.

Courtesy of COVAD. Reprinted with permission.

On TV, whispering can mean turning down the volume and slowing down the video. During the 1999 holiday season, online retailer buy.com ran 30-second TV spots in San Francisco that consisted of nothing but the words "buy.com" superimposed in white letters on a black screen. No motion, no video, no announcer, no volume—nothing but the words. This spot was so striking that the ad was unavoidable if your were in the room when it came on. This whisper practically roared. Marketing professionals may justly criticize the spot as yet another example of meaningless dot-com advertising, but purely in terms of getting attention, it succeeded.

Newspapers are the most visually cluttered of all the media. Some newspaper advertisers turn this disadvantage into an advantage by creating small messages inside great expanses of unfilled white space. These whispering ads are extremely effective in attracting attention by virtue of their marked contrast to the hustle and bustle of the surrounding pages.

Although the Ford Motor Company paid millions to sponsor the U.S. television premiere of Steven Spielberg's *Schindler's List*, the company limited commercial interruptions to a minimum. Given the gravity of the holocaust subject matter, and despite the premium price tag, whispering was the only dignified way to approach advertising within such an environment. Ford received widespread praise for its courage and its understated treatment.

Paradoxically, within an exceptionally noisy and cluttered setting, a whisper can seem louder than a shout—engaging us, intriguing us, and pulling us in. That was the idea behind the campaign we produced for MGM Grand. In Las Vegas, MGM Grand operates one of the largest and most extravagant casinos and hotels in the world. If any town stands for noise, glitz, and flash, it's Las Vegas. But our ads for the MGM Grand weren't designed to shout above the ambient noise. Rather, they were designed to attract with a whisper.

For the hotel's spa, we crafted TV and outdoor ads that were in counterpoint to the character of Las Vegas. Las Vegas is *loud*. These ads are quiet. Las Vegas is *exciting*. These ads are relaxing. Las Vegas wants to *draw you in*. These ads want you to escape. These weren't ads so much as antidotes to the overwhelming sensation of Las Vegas.

This ad for the MGM Grand spa whispers to get attention.

Courtesy of MGM Grand. Reprinted with permission.

# Playing Hard to Get and Teasing

Playing hard to get or teasing are variations on the whispering theme. In a recent study, Satya Menon of the University of Chicago and Dilip Somon of the University of Colorado at Boulder found that these strategies can be particularly effective for two kinds of marketers: (1) technology marketers with radically new products that incorporate unfamiliar innovations (digital cameras, personal video recorders, WebTV, etc.) and (2) Internet marketers who must entice users to activate banner ads. In their report, "Managing Consumer Motivation and Learning: Harnessing the Power of Curiosity for Effective Advertising Strategies," Menon and Somon outline why these strategies work: *Curiosity is a powerful thing.* Ads that pique interest but don't reveal the whole story increase consumers' motivation to learn more—even if the product is complicated. Hinting and teasing draw in consumers and make them hungry to learn more. They will pay some attention to satisfy their curiosity.

## Curiosity-Arousing Street Theater

During the summer of 1999, About.com (formerly the Mining Company) generated a lot of curiosity with its tease campaign, headlined "Hello, is anybody out there?" For several weeks, outdoor boards in New York, Los Angeles, and San Francisco, along with print ads in selected newspapers, carried this cryptic but unexplained message.

The campaign culminated with highly effective street theater. Bizarrely costumed characters holding placards with the "Hello" message greeted morning commuters at high-traffic off-ramps and commuter stations. There was nothing high tech about it, but the tease achieved its desired effect. I can personally attest to numerous "Hey, did you see that . . . I wonder who's doing that . . ." conversations in San Francisco during the campaign. The *Wall Street Journal* even published a story with the scoop that the teaser was, in fact, About.com.

Lee Jeans employed a variation of a teasing strategy when it launched its hard-to-get 1998 Lee dungarees campaign.

Lee found that its targeted consumers, 17- to 25-year-olds, are turned off by the hard-selling wiles of advertisers. In research for the campaign,

About.com getting attention on the street . . . "Hello, is anybody out there?"

Courtesy of About.com. Reprinted with permission.

these young but sophisticated consumers said, "The harder you try, the more we are *not* going to pay attention to your brand." That led agency Fallon McElligott to develop the "Buddy Lee" campaign.

> Buddy Lee is a doll that was used by Lee as a promotional item in the 1920s. In March of 1998, posters went up in 15 cities showing just the surreal-looking doll and an enigmatic piece of small print: MOA #2. In May of that year, night owls might have caught the six-minute short film on Comedy Central—it ran at 1 A.M.—that explained the origins of Buddy Lee and his connection to Lee's new product, Dungarees. It also explained that MOA means Man of Action. The idea is to let just a few people in on the joke and let the ads' meaning filter out by word of mouth. Leading-edge kids like to feel like they are in the know.[1]

A more recent, and more celebrated, hard-to-get approach was successfully adopted by the marketers of the summer of 1999's surprise movie hit, *The Blair Witch Project*. Artisan Entertainment, *Blair Witch's* distributor and marketer, evidently took Sir Winston Churchill's words to heart: "We have no money, so we shall have to think."

Lacking big-studio marketing budgets, Artisan shunned expensive TV ads in favor of web sites and screenings on college campuses. Then, when the film premiered, it opened on so few screens that relatively few viewers could see it at any one time. The movie began selling out weeks in advance. "People do have the experience of going and not being able to get in . . . what we're doing is creating that buzz factor on film. If you want to be in the know, if you want to be in the right place at the right time, you should be seeing *Blair Witch*."[2]

# Viral Marketing: Word of Mouth

*Viral marketing* is the fashionable name for what used to be known as plain old word-of-mouth ("recruit-a-friend") advertising. Viral marketers use their existing customers to recruit new ones. Messages spread virally can multiply rapidly. Many believe that word of mouth is the most powerful form of marketing communication. A personal recommendation from a friend, relative, or colleague can supersede millions of dollars spent through conventional marketing channels. Some of the web's most powerful brand names—Yahoo!, Amazon, and many others—were built largely by word of mouth.

In a recent study, DiMassimo Brand Advertising found that inaccuracies and deceptions spread by word of mouth can erase the impact of millions of dollars of ad spending. For example, just because "someone said so," 27% of those in the study were convinced that "Just do it" was the slogan, not of Nike, but of Ex-Lax.

Viral marketing has been employed with great effect by many web marketers. For example, Hotmail and several other e-mail providers offer free service to users if they allow ad banners to be placed on their messages. One banner recruits new users, so every time I send one of these e-mails, I am recruiting my intended recipient to join the service as well. Epidemic Marketing Inc. goes even further—this e-mail provider *pays* users to attach its ads to their e-mail messages.

Yahoo! uses creative street theater as a catalyst for word-of-mouth advertising. The company engineers events to put a "human face on this otherwise virtual brand," according to Karen Edwards, vice president of brand marketing. For example, Yahoo! hired people to dress as chauffeurs and stand around airports holding signs that read: "No, I'm not waiting for anyone . . . just want you to try travel.yahoo.com." The goal is to get people talking so that they can influence others. Luanne Calvert, whose title at Yahoo! is Buzz Marketer, gathers event ideas from everyone at Yahoo! and its ad agency, Black Rocket, and then implements the programs.

Other online business models compensate participants for customer referrals. The more people you sign up, the more you get paid. Cookexpress (which used the web to market home delivery of ready-to-cook gourmet meals) gave customers $20 discounts if they steered friends to the Cookexpress web site. Eight percent of the referrals became loyal buyers who then recruited even more customers.

Many shopping web sites employ a form of electronic word of mouth. They use bots and collaborative filtering technologies to create "recommendation engines" that can produce highly tailored and personalized suggestions on what to buy.

Yahoo!, directing buzz at SFO.

Viral marketing, playing hard to get, teasing—all are ways to whisper rather than shout. And whispering is one of several building blocks for attention mechanics.

# Finding a Quieter Place

Sometimes, standing in the midst of the throng makes it nearly impossible to command attention in a crowded room. Let's say you're recovering from the flu, you've got a sore throat, and you just can't scream loud enough to distract people from what they're doing. At times like this, a good strategy would be to find a quieter place to stand—a part of the room that's less noisy and crowded, where even with your sore throat you'd stand at least a chance of getting someone's attention.

Finding a quieter place is one of the easiest ways to draw attention, and it's surprising that it's not employed more often. For brands, quiet places could be windows of time during which competitors are typically dormant. Quiet places could be types of media that competitors usually avoid. Within media types, quiet places could be programs, issues, or vehicles that competitors seldom use to advertise.

## Dealing with Clutter

Quiet places can also be low-clutter media—TV shows, magazines, cable channels, and so on that are less heavily advertised in general. On broadcast television, ABC, CBS, and NBC prime-time programs are still considered the advertising "gold standard" by many marketers—the best means to achieve mass reach among attentive prospects. Yet even here, advertising clutter has been rising unabated since tracking began.

Currently, about 16 minutes of every broadcast prime-time program hour are devoted to nonprogram interruptions—commercials, promotional announcements, and so on. For daytime TV, the situation is even worse—one-third of every broadcast daytime hour carries nonprogram matter. Numerous studies reveal the impact of this trend: Commercial recall scores are declining, and audience levels, already reduced by media fragmentation, have greatly diminished during commercial breaks.

Clutter is increasing.

## Non-program minutes per hour–primetime, 4 nets

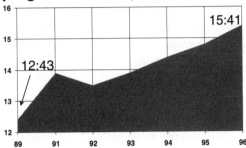

AAAA/ANA 1996 TV Communication Monitoring Report (November data)

At my firm, we are exploring a variety of techniques to mitigate the impact of clutter:

- *We're taking attention into account when we plan and buy media.* This is important because traditional audience surveys (e.g., the Nielsen ratings) are not designed to report whether anyone is actually pay- ing attention to a program or an ad. Most ratings research counts *opportunities*, not actualities. And the same is true for non-TV audi- ence surveys. The standard in the industry today is often described as "opportunity to see," or "opportunity to hear." Survey firms mea- sure whether audiences had a chance to be exposed to media, not whether they actually were, and further, if they were, whether they paid attention. It takes specialized studies to put attention in the spotlight.
- *We're using exposure values to adjust media audience ratings.* Since sur- vey firms do not routinely measure attention, we have to adjust accordingly. One way we do this is by using exposure values. Expo- sure values help us get a more realistic picture of the size of the atten- tive audience for our ad. Exposure values are our educated guesses (based on best available research). Exposure values represent the pro- portion of the rated audience that actually was exposed to an ad (as

opposed to the lower standard of having an opportunity to be exposed). For example, if Nielsen reports that a program is viewed by 20 million people, and our exposure value for the show is 50%, we estimate the *attentive* audience to be 10 million, not the 20 million reported in the survey. By applying these factors to rated audience figures, we can strip away the nonproductive, inattentive chaff from the attentive wheat.

- *We're steering clients away from low-attention media environments.* We are discouraging clients from using highly cluttered programs or middle-of-the-pod commercial positions and steering them toward high-attention and exclusive-advertiser media environments.

- *By using low-attention media, we expect to pay less accordingly.* We're taking attention into account during our media pricing negotiations.

## Avoiding the Baked-in Bias

Earlier, I mentioned that "baked-in media biases" are prevalent in my industry: packaged goods for TV, retail for newspapers and radio, print for high-tech products (with a sprinkling of online), and so on. Brands that break out of their baked-in biases can attract attention with surprisingly little effort.

One of my favorite examples of finding a quieter place is the ongoing campaign for Altoids "curiously strong" breath mints—basically just candy. A traditional candy advertiser's media plan would have anchored itself nationally in late-afternoon television to reach kids as well as moms, to exploit the pang for a predinner snack, and perhaps to catch folks prior to a late-afternoon shopping trip.

But Altoids shunned national ads to concentrate on just a few markets, rejecting TV in favor of bus shelters, outdoor boards, subway ads, and alternative weekly newspapers. The whole strategy focused on the words *curious* and *strong* with intriguing depictions (e.g., a bodybuilder squeezing a can of Altoids, headlined, "Nice altoids"), each on a lime-green background. Altoids new campaign ad budget was reportedly a mere $1 million in its first year, but sales leaped 30 percent. A small budget can go a long way in a quieter place.

On a somewhat larger budgetary scale, General Motors recently saw fit to exploit a quieter place itself—no small irony given its $2 billion ad

Altoids found a quieter place by adopting a novel media strategy.

Courtesy of Altoids. Reprinted with permission.

budget. GM began promoting its association with the year 2000 Olympic Games by running ads in June 1999, 15 months before the games began. Observes GM's vice president of advertising Phil Guarascio, "You can shout louder than everyone else when everyone else is doing it—which is very inefficient—or you can start when your voice is most prominent, which is most effective from a spending standpoint."[3]

Along similar lines, Mont Blanc, retailer of high-end office supplies, recently installed a "De-acceleration Studio" inside its New York boutique retail location. It is intended to be an untroubled oasis of calm, a place to stop the world for a moment and contemplate . . . not far from the buzzing cash registers.

## Windows of Opportunity

One way to whisper is to seek out quieter places within your brand's competitive set. Quieter places are times (months, weeks, days, or hours) and places (regions, markets, neighborhoods, and other venues) when and where sales potential is strong but category advertising noise has been historically light:

For a hotel chain that caters to business travelers, an ad in *USA Today* may encounter a lot of competitive noise. An ad in *Sports Illustrated* might represent a quieter place.

For a corporate-image business-to-business campaign, a spot on *Meet the Press* may be surrounded by like-minded commercials. A spot on *Biography* might reside in a quieter place.

These examples represent underexploited windows of opportunity. Some of the substantial effort that is usually spent defining the target audience should instead be directed to discovering windows of opportunity—situations that represent low noise and high relevance. Even light levels of advertising can yield a powerful effect when the window is open.

One way to identify an open window for the future is to examine an

**Find your windows of opportunity.**

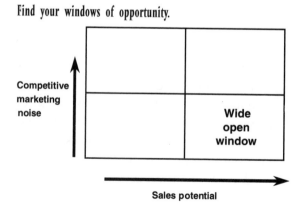

Competitive marketing noise

Wide open window

Sales potential

open window in the past. Although not a sure predictor, historical spending patterns for competitive media, especially those in the recent past, are surprisingly repetitive. Some spending characteristics are baked into a company's budgeting processes ("June is the last month of our fiscal year . . . we always cancel media in June if our numbers are soft"). Others are predicated on long-standing business cycles or geographical distribution dynamics. At my firm, we've developed a proprietary tool for predicting windows of opportunity. Based on statistical modeling of historical data, it's given us an accurate read on the future more than a few times.

Quieter places can also mean venues where a product's message is unexpected but highly relevant and thus strongly memorable: an ad for a limousine service on a luggage carousel at the airport (the pre-taxi "daypart"), an ad sticker for ABC's yellow-hued "TV is good" campaign on a banana at the supermarket (the yellow "daypart"), an ad for a morning newspaper on gourmet coffee cups (the morning-jolt "daypart").

For a hotel chain that was trying to burnish its fading image, we once recommended a "fashion/badge brand" media strategy: Advertise the hotel as a fashion brand in *Vanity Fair* and *Vogue* instead of *USA Today* and the *Wall Street Journal*. Use giant wallscapes in world crossroads locations instead of spreads in *Fortune* and *Business Week*.

We once recommended that an airplane manufacturer focus its entire advertising budget in and around the one environment frequented by all of its target constituencies—the airport.

Debuting every day are new media forms that can deliver messages in highly relevant ways. Turner Broadcasting is launching a mall network aimed at teen girls in battle-ready shopping mode. The network is replete with wall monitors, interactive media stations, web sites, and a magazine.

For a restaurant chain, ad panels in hotel elevators carry messages on a mirror with the headline, "You look hungry." TV monitors attached to bicycles offer advertisers an outdoor video network—a movable feast of impromptu TV ads.

When the relevance of the message is enhanced by the medium delivering it, the sense is not one of unwelcome intrusion but of helpful advice.

As with whispering, finding a quieter place is becoming an effective counterstrategy to the swelling cacophony of the media space.

# 9

# Be Different

To get attention, you really have to be different.
*Scott Sassa*, The Wall Street Journal, *January 15, 1999*

Whispering and finding a quieter place are examples of contrarian approaches to getting attention. These sorts of behaviors call attention to themselves precisely because they are so different from the prevailing behaviors. And being different is critical if we're serious about getting attention. Evolution has hardwired our brains to pay close attention to what's different—because what's different might be a predator or prey.

## The Cocktail Party Effect

Getting attention in a crowded room need not be an all-or-nothing affair. The literature of cognitive psychology has long recognized a phenomenon called the *cocktail party effect*.

We tend to think that we are good at concentrating on only one thing at a time. But scientific studies on perception in situations with low signal-to-noise ratios (high noise, low signal) show that, in some circumstances, we can effectively monitor two or more separate streams of information simultaneously. People at a cocktail party (the classic example of a crowded room) often follow one conversation and tune out the surrounding ones—*until* the surrounding conversations pique their interest!

Web surfers are quite familiar with the cocktail party effect. According to a 1999 study by NPD in conjunction with Iconocast, 57% of U.S. web users multitask—that is, they surf the web and watch TV simultaneously.

In a recent paper on the effect, MIT Media Lab researcher Barry Arons evoked principles of Gestalt psychology to explain the cocktail party effect. According to Arons, the features of messages that attract attention (i.e., make messages stand out in the sensory field) as opposed to those that repel attention (i.e., make messages blend into the sensory field) are as follows:

| Attract Attention | Repel Attention |
|---|---|
| Dissimilarity | Similarity |
| Separateness | Proximity |
| Discontinuity | Continuity |
| Uncommonality | Commonality |
| Asymmetry | Symmetry |

Clearly, differentiation, and distinctiveness are critical if we want to register a message, particularly a marketing message. If it's not different, it won't break through. Being different is one of the most powerful ways of standing out.

Differentiation is also a powerful route to competitive advantage. Legendary Coca-Cola marketer Roberto Goizueta attributed his brand's enduring success to differentiation, pure and simple:

> If the three keys to selling real estate are location, location, location, then the three keys of selling consumer products are differentiation, differentiation, differentiation. In recent years, we can honestly say that every marketing victory we have won has been the result of our total commitment to making our brands clearly distinctive from every other item on the grocery shelf . . . The most notable action has been our ongoing expansion of the famous trademarked contour bottle throughout the entire world-wide packaging line for Coca-Cola, arguably the

single most effective differentiation effort the soft drink industry has seen in many years.[1]

## Differentiated Brand Propositions

For brand marketers, being different means seizing a differentiated brand proposition and focusing all marketing communications single-mindedly around it. A brand proposition is the sun around which we want all marketing messages to orbit. It's the idea that sets the brand apart from all of its competitors. A brand proposition is not the only statement a brand needs to make, but it is the most important one. Brand propositions wedge open the door to the consumer's mind. If successful, brand propositions are conversation starters.

Volvo's brand proposition has historically been anchored in *safety*, Lysol's in *disinfection*, Federal Express's in *absolutely, positively overnight!*, and so on.

To extract the maximum return on their communications investments, marketers should make certain that their brand's proposition is front and center in all elements of the marketing mix—not just in creative executions, but in media plans, public relations, sales promotions, direct marketing, packaging, and so on. All messages should reinforce the brand's basic selling proposition.

Young & Rubicam's campaign for Chevron gasoline is an excellent example of a powerfully differentiated brand proposition extended throughout the communications spectrum. To many consumers, gasoline is a commodity, the only loyalty is to low prices, and the experience of filling the tank is an unpleasant, though unavoidable, necessity. Surveys show that not only do consumers have a low interest in gasoline, but gasoline advertising is one of the most actively avoided of all advertising categories. In fact, it ranks down near the bottom (right next to insurance advertising).

And yet, today Chevron enjoys unparalleled customer loyalty. The reason: Chevron is a highly effective brand proposition marketer.

Chevron's World of Cars campaign is the highest scoring in gasoline history.

Reprinted with permission of Chevron Corporation.

To arrive at their selling proposition, Chevron and Young & Rubicam's Charlie McQuilken, John O'Meara, and Peter Angelos looked at gasoline in a completely different way: It is cars, not people, who have to drink the stuff. Who better to be spokespeople (spokescars?) for the gasoline? Who better to tell the story of the proposition, "Chevron is the gasoline that makes cars happy"?

The story of how Chevron makes cars happy started on TV with a series of highly engaging talking-car commercials (the highest-scoring TV commercials in the history of gasoline advertising, according to copy research firms). It extended to radio, magazines, newspapers, and outdoor billboards. It extended onto web sites and online campaigns. It extended throughout the service station with signage, collateral material, even uniform patches. It extended into an ancillary sales opportunity through toy car sales and other sales of campaign-related merchandise. Chevron, its managers now proudly proclaim, sells more cars each year than Ford or General Motors. It has even extended into rides at Disneyland.

## Disrupting Conventions

If marketers aren't careful, it's easy for their brands to slip off consumers' radar screens. Most of us are on information overload. If we have already established a view of a particular brand, we might screen out redundant ads. We don't have room for superfluous information. We ignore it. We zap it. We screen it out.

If consumer perceptions about a brand are *wrong*, then its marketers are in trouble and may need to disrupt the established view and overturn the conventional opinions. Brands that are in the process of disrupting conventions are noticeably different. Disrupting conventions can be powerful ways to get attention. (Jean-Marie Dru wrote the classic book on this topic, *Disruption*, published by John Wiley & Sons.)

We at Young & Rubicam confronted a similar situation several years ago while working with our Ford client (Ford/Mercury Dealers Group) in Canada. Ford's sales were soft and not improving fast enough. One reason was that some Canadians had an established opinion about Ford that was wrong: They viewed Fords as cheap, unexciting cars. Not luxurious. Not high-performing. Not sexy like the imports. Boring but serviceable.

The facts did not support this view. Ford cars were not bland and boring. Their engineering, performance, and luxury characteristics were competitive with the imports. But getting that story across to people who believed differently was a tough task. The straightforward approach wouldn't work. Ads that simply stated the facts would be screened out ("Don't confuse me with the facts! I know what I know"). That situation was unacceptable to us and to Ford. To break through with our message, we developed a disruption strategy of our own called "Denial, Acceptance, and Love." These were the three phases of our ad campaign.

In phase 1 (Denial), we ran a blitz of TV commercials that were disruptive *because they admitted the obvious*. People thought Ford's cars were boring, and these commercials were designed to show people saying just that. Interviewers stopped passersby on Toronto streets and asked if they'd test-drive a Ford Probe (in one commercial) or Ford Explorer (in another). Most of the footage consisted of people resisting the invitation with candid remarks—some of the kindest words tended to be of the "absolutely not" variety, but harsher remarks were recorded as well. For an entire month, Ford ran these ads. That took guts. But it got attention and started a buzz.

In phase 2 (Acceptance), we followed up with TV commercials that demonstrated a softening in people's attitudes. Passersby who actually walked over to the Ford cars we had parked by the roadside now had guarded, but positive, things to say: "That's a Ford?" "That's a nice looking car!" For a month, we saturated the airwaves with these phase 2 spots. We were gaining credibility fast. We had earned some trust.

In phase 3 (Love), we shifted the emphasis to people's spontaneous and candid reactions to their test-driving experience. Drivers were ecstatic. Ford's cars beat every expectation for comfort and performance. People gushed with litanies of superlatives. Their enthusiasm was believable because we had been brutally honest throughout the entire process.

This campaign worked well for Ford. It won the 1993 Bessie Award for best Canadian ad campaign of the year. But more important, it attracted the attention of consumers. It got people talking. It got Ford back on people's consideration lists when they shopped for cars. It was different because it disrupted conventions.

An invitation to be different is *not* a license to be stupid. "We want you to remember our name: Outpost.com. That's why we've decided to fire gerbils out of this cannon." This was the opening line for a recent debutant dot-com's TV commercial. The electronics retailer has since switched messages, since, according to CEO Bob Bowman, "Our brand has to stand for something, and it can't stand for gerbils."

This three-phase Ford campaign took guts to air.

| denial | acceptence | love |

A Lincoln?.... No.

I used to think it was an old man's car.

Listen. You can't even hear it go! Honestly you can't even hear the engine. This is wonderful.

Ma'am? Would you like to...

That's a nice lookin' car.

Feels great. Handles great. Better than the Zamboni.

I don't go for American cars. They're too big.

It's got a lovely front, look at all the buttons.

Really hugs those corners. That's fantastic, eh?

Courtesy of Young & Rubicam, Toronto. Reprinted with permission.

The gerbils ploy might actually look tasteful compared to some other dot-com TV commercials: For Cyberian Outpost, ferocious wolves attack a high-school marching band. For Buy.com, a man kneels down to sniff a dog's butt. For CNET, someone is getting a proctological exam. For AltaVista, a guy drops his cell phone into a urinal. Just-hatched dot-com brands seem to have appeared out of nowhere and sometimes seem to dominate the airwaves. Ad reviewer Bob Garfield put it nicely: "Everywhere you look, the press is noticing that dot-com advertising is everywhere you look."

Despite their ubiquity, offline ads for many dot-coms just aren't registering. According to a study by Active Research of San Francisco, 25 percent of those surveyed couldn't remember a single dot-com ad they had seen, much less associate it with the correct advertiser. TV ads for Etoys, one of the leaders in the study, were recalled by only 3% of viewers—far below the 15 to 30% norms.

And, to prove that dot-coms have not cornered the market on meaningless drivel, Adidas once ran a print ad that featured a guy blowing snot out of his nose. Outlandish slogans, offensive displays, and shocking images are poor foundations for building strong and enduring brands.

Strong brands are even more important in today's fragmented marketing environment than they were in the past. A hundred years ago, Ivory soap came in one form and was sold through one channel—the general store. Today Ivory soap exists in over 100 forms and is sold through countless channels in every region of the world. Only the brand endures unchanged.

A relevant, single-minded, and highly differentiated brand proposition, is critical if brands are serious about getting and holding the consumer's attention.

## Artists versus Engineers

In advertising, as in many other endeavors, there is an engineering dimension and an artistic dimension. The engineering dimension is the domain of most quantitative research, testing, experimentation, modeling, proprietary tools, systems, and so on. Some of the most powerful tools (e.g., models and software optimizers) are also the most expensive. Only the largest agencies can compete effectively in the engineering domain because only they can afford the best and latest tools. The engineering dimension employs all of its mechanical muscle to eke out usually small (though not insignificant) improvements in communications performance.

The artistic dimension has few tools and systems. It's not (at least conventionally) expensive. But unquestionably it holds, and always will hold, the only promise of producing a quantum leap in communications performance (as opposed to the incremental gains delivered by the engineers). The reason is that the artistic dimension is centered around *ideas*.

In the media planning arena, the developments attracting the most notoriety recently have had to do with the engineering dimension—with much of the press attention focused on million-dollar optimizer software. These engineering tools are laudable because they can deliver modest improvements in plan performance. But for really large improvements, at my firm we turn our attention elsewhere.

## POP

When developing media plans, we employ a technique called *primary organizing principle* (POP) to create truly different media plans. For us, an effective POP fits three criteria: (1) It's a simple media idea (not veiled in industry jargon like *reach* or *impact*); (2) it sets the brand apart from competitors; and (3) it strategically resonates with the brand's selling proposition. POPs propel us toward media strategies that are quantum leaps beyond anything our engineering tools can produce. In fact, the best POPs lead us to places where engineering tools could never take us.

One of my favorite POPs was for one of our smallest brands—Diamond Walnuts, which is a baking ingredient. The traditional so-called optimally engineered media plan for Diamond Walnuts would have targeted women who bake by running recipe ads in cooking magazines, with a liberal dose of supplemental ads during daytime TV (notoriously efficient for reaching women). Some variation on that theme would have been the best plan media science could produce. But our POP led us in a completely different direction.

For Diamond Walnuts, the POP that emerged, "Link Diamond Walnuts with warm holiday memories," was based on our memories. People tend to vividly recall the holiday times when they were growing up. A surprising number of us have a childhood memory of our baking "assistance" being rewarded by a lick of the spoon used to stir the batter. Most of these memories emanate from a very specific point in time—basically the 30 days between Thanksgiving and Christmas when most baking occurs in the United States. In creative executions and in our media plan, we wanted to link Diamond Walnuts to this special time and place in people's memories.

We avoided recipe ads in magazines and daytime TV. We used primarily evening TV focused around Thanksgiving and Christmas. We sponsored every holiday special and movie we could find. We splurged on holiday programming—the Macy's parade, the 500th showing of Bing Crosby's *White Christmas*, the reprise of James Stewart's *It's a Wonderful Life*, and so on. Beyond TV, we were always looking for additional media tie-ins with a holiday theme (sponsoring *Nutcracker* ballet performances, running ads in programs, etc.).

This POP became a successful strategy for Diamond Walnuts for many years. It worked because it was different.

Kraft Foods' Altoids brand of mints is another example of a strong central idea driving the marketing communications plan in new directions. Chris Peddy, senior brand manager for Altoids, describes its POP this way: Altoids mints are curious, strong, and original. Altoids' goal is to surprise and delight consumers with things that are curious, strong, and original. This simple idea has given rise to a cornucopia of unique, but strategically focused, attention-getting ploys, from sponsoring the Curiously Strong Art Collection, a program which supports and exhibits the work of emerging visual artists, to wrapping a building at O'Hare airport to look like the shape of the Altoids tin.

Another way to think differently is to *think with your entire budget*. Media innovator Chris Whittle used to tell a story to illustrate the importance of being bold. Our brands could be truly different if only we would, in his words, "think with our whole budget." I don't remember the particulars, but his story went something like this.

General Motors spends over $2 billion a year advertising cars in the United States. Do you know how many people actually buy a new car in the United States every year? A surprisingly small number . . . only a few million. If General Motors thought with its whole budget, it could eliminate all its TV and print ads and do something much more dramatic. With that huge budget, GM could take every U.S. prospect to the Four Seasons restaurant for lunch and give them a personal sales pitch.

Perhaps not an effective idea . . . put perhaps so. The point is, we may miss out on the boldest, most distinctive ideas unless we are willing to relinquish our conventions and think with our whole budget.

# 10

# Touch

We seem to have lost the ability to communicate humanely and intelligently at the precise moment we have a mind-boggling array of devices designed to shove information . . .

*Jon Carroll*, San Francisco Chronicle, *August 6, 1999*

To return to our crowded room, one surefire way to get attention is to walk up to people and touch them. Touching is one of the most effective ways to grab attention. Being touched is hard to ignore.

Attention mechanics uses many techniques to initiate communication, but none is more powerful than touch. Ironically, touching (i.e., a face-to-face encounter) is gaining communications power in direct proportion to the rise and penetration of pseudo-touching technologies (e-mail, voice mail, teleconferencing, instant messaging, etc.). But even the most powerful communications technologies for customizing, personalizing, and offering one-on-one messages will not take the place of personal encounters in marketing communications.

One shrewd observer of the modern media scene, Michael Schrage, recently opined that personalization has in itself become a commodity—something we've come to expect on every web site today, MyYahoo, MyExcite, MyCrowdedRoomMetaphor.

## Personal Contact

Psychologist Steven Pinker has a theory that personal, face-to-face encounters—trade shows, conferences, seminars, personal business meetings—will never become obsolete. The need to preserve face-to-face meetings will necessitate ongoing corporate expense. And that expense will continue to support entire industries—hotels, airlines, rental cars, and so on. And why is this so? Because, according to Pinker, we can't trust people until we meet them in the flesh, until we see "what makes them sweat."

Edward Hallowell, a psychiatrist at Harvard Medical School, has written about the need we have in our business relationships to experience what he calls "the human moment," an authentic encounter that has two prerequisites: (1) people's physical presence in a shared space and (2) their emotional and intellectual attention.

The more technologically based our communications infrastructure becomes, the more we will crave touch. As more activities move online, dealings with other humans will grow in importance. It's easy to see why when we examine how people really behave. Take the example of Darcia and Betty.

Darcia is a customer service representative for Lands' End. Betty is a Lands' End customer. Their interaction on a recent fall day was chronicled by author Malcolm Gladwell in *The New Yorker*[1]:

> Betty was browsing the Lands' End web site for a pair of sweatpants suitable for her young daughter. She couldn't decide what to get, so she called Darcia.

*Betty:* What size did I order last year? I think I need one size bigger.

*Darcia:* Last year, you bought the same pants in big-kids' small.

*Betty:* I'm thinking medium or large.

*Darcia:* The medium is a ten or twelve, really closer to a twelve. I'm thinking that if you go to a large, it will throw you up to a sixteen, which is really big.

*Betty:*   I agree. I want the medium. By the way, I need the pants by Tuesday.

*Darcia:*  With second-day air, you will almost certainly get the package by Tuesday.

*Betty:*   How much does next-day delivery cost?

*Darcia:*  Premium next-day delivery service is available for six dollars, but are you sure you need that? It's only an eighteen-dollar order.

*Betty:*   Thanks. I'll stay with second-day air.

Betty hung up, and completed her transaction online. (Although I have abridged some of the dialogue, the exchange is accurate.) Clearly, the Lands' End web site is not putting customer service reps out of business. The human interaction closed the sale. Betty's last-minute doubts and anxieties exhibited normal shopping behavior. By reassuring Betty that her daughter was a medium, not a large, Darcia clinched the order. The Internet is not self-service like a gas station. The sales process can never be completely automated. People need some hand-holding. Occasionally, they need to "touch."

Gladwell goes on to describe how all of Lands' End's sales channels (800 number, catalog, web site) are intertwined. For example, when the company mails out new catalogs, one might expect that web site orders would decline as people switch over to ordering by telephone. Paradoxically, the reverse is true. When a new catalog arrives, web orders spike. The retailer has found that people often shop the web site with the catalog at hand.

Columnist Michael Schrage predicts that "odds are excellent that future human interactions will revolve around the failure of technology to do what the customer wants."[2] In a recent survey by NFO interactive, 35% of online shoppers would buy more online if they could communicate with a person on the other end.

Pure e-commerce, conducted without live human intervention, will always have limits. Imagine what it would be like to walk into a department store without employees. The shelves and racks might be well-stocked, but our impulse to buy would be much curtailed. No one would be there to point out a new item we might like. No one would be there to answer our questions about washing instructions for a fragile-looking garment. No one would give us a time frame for that back-ordered sweater in the deep purple color our uncle adores. Most shoppers need to talk to a salesperson at least sometimes.

It seems as if it is human nature to yearn for the past. Since the past cannot be obtained, it is human nature to create idealized versions of the past. Megan Santosus, senior editor at CIO Enterprise magazine concurs. "If anything, e-commerce promises to return us to the days when the milkman delivered a daily quart and the Fuller Brush guy stopped in once a month."[3]

Our suburban homes are designed to bring to mind the nineteenth-century farm, with our yards as the pastures and fields. Our malls and our suburban shopping centers reminiscent of downtown open-air markets (like the one near my home in Walnut Creek, California) recall nineteenth-century Main Street. We yearn for the one-on-one marketing of the good old days—personal, face-to-face encounters with merchants who know us well and understand our needs. (Some of us can still find vestiges of the real thing in the form of a good butcher!)

In a recent roundtable discussion, Allan Falvey of Warner-Lambert traced the history of grocery shopping:

> If you look at the history of the industry in the last 100 years, you'll notice that there's a pendulum that tends to come back to a marketing balance. Brand marketing as we know it today started out with little boutique stores. High levels of customer service and a lot of direct-to-consumer interaction. We grew up with the bread truck and the milk truck that used to deliver bread and milk. Today, I could have been describing the Internet. A lot of boutique marketing, a lot of direct-to-consumer, a lot of customer service. And if you look at the patterns of marketing over the last 100 years, you'll see that pendulum seems to swing back and forth between individualization and consolidation. You could go through each decade and see where that has had its effect. Usually, it's technology driven.[4]

Touch is a powerful technique of attention mechanics. Entire marketing strategies have evolved around touching the consumer. One example is Manhattan-based Kiehl's. In the worlds of fashion and entertainment, where fame is parceled out in nanoseconds, Kiehl's, a 149-year-old maker of hair and skin-care products, is *hot*. Movie stars such as Winona Ryder and Sarah Jessica Parker swear by its products. Giant cosmetic firms have made overtures to buy Kiehl's. Fashion arbiters *Vogue* and *Marie Claire* cite Kiehl's as among the best available.

So, what accounts for Kiehl's great success? Advertising? No, Kiehl's doesn't. E-commerce? No, Kiehl's doesn't. Public relations? No, Kiehl's doesn't. Bold packaging? No, Kiehl's packages are plain (mostly small type on white paper). Broad distribution? No, Kiehl's has only one retail store, in Manhattan's East Village. Outside of this store, Kiehl's products are sold only in the world's most exclusive department stores.

The secret to Kiehl's success is that the company touches its customers. It lavishes attention on them. It is not unusual for staff to spend half an hour with a single customer, even if a long line of devotees is waiting. During these extended consultations, Kiehl's is an aggressive sampler, giving away huge quantities of its products to anyone who comes into the store—to the tune of $1.5 million worth of free merchandise each year. Salesclerks are encouraged to give out samples, not to make sales. According to Jamie Morse, co-owner of Kiehl's, "Touching a person—that's the best way to make a business grow."[5]

## Online Chat, Live Help

Web technologists find ways to overcome most challenges, even inventing mechanical ways to deliver a human touch. Some are ingenious. Several firms (Webline Communications, LivePerson, PeopleSupport, NewsChannel) offer a Live Help button that triggers a pop-up chat box (similar to AOL's Instant Messaging system). Users can type in a question or request and get an immediate typed response from a live rep, who can, if needed, go the further step of telephoning the user.

NewChannel enables a firm's customer service personnel to engage in live chat as well, but its system has sophisticated features such as filters and rules that govern chat boxes (e.g., to appear only on certain pages, only at certain times, and only for certain users).

But no technological tinkering can replace the real thing: Sometimes, to get attention, we need to touch. It is analogous to what American social philosopher Lewis Mumford once wrote about our form of government: "Democracy, in any active sense, begins and ends in communities small enough for their members to meet face-to-face." Allow customers to touch your brand's organization by talking with them or meeting them face-to-face at key points along the consideration path.

# 11

# Tell a Story

It's been a long time since I've read of anything that's in short supply. Do you know of anything?

Attention.

*Leon Levy and Walter Wriston, Interview in* Forbes. *March 8, 1999*

In a crowded room, the people most likely monopolizing attention are the storytellers. They are the focus of the clique. People press in to hear the joke they're telling or the gossip they're relating. Storytellers are irresistable. They can get attention any time, any place.

People have always been suckers for stories. We understand the world through stories. In marketing communications, it is useful to think that our brand has a story to tell as well. It could be a very long story with many twists and turns. Or it could be short. Each time out, the brand may relate only one episode in a longer narrative. But the longer story exists, and, over time, it will be told, embellished, amended, and expanded. "Successful future brands will regard themselves as stories," agrees Kevin Roberts, CEO of Saatchi & Saatchi in London. "The heroes of these stories will be anything—products, services personalities—even attitudes."[1]

For example, say our brand is Hercules. One ad is going to tell the story of how our brand cleaned the Augean stables ("tough on stains")! The next ad is going to tell the story of how our brand dispatched the Hydra of Lerna ("powers out dirt and odors")! Our Hercules brand has a long story to tell, but we need not tell it all at once.

In the marketing world, brands have many stories they need to tell. Stories about functionality, about values, about how one brand in the franchise family relates to another.

Apple's story is about its ongoing struggle to release people from the tyranny of conventional computers. Nike's story is about how it can help each one of us, no matter what our circumstances, become confident athletes. Chevron's story is about its concern for cars and doing whatever it takes to make them happy.

Stories offer fast access to something even more powerful than our rational minds: our *emotions*. Although customers rationalize with facts, they decide with emotions. According to neurologist Antonio Damasio, emotions are the primary means by which we become aware of our needs and determine how we will satisfy them.

At Nike, where executives place a high premium on brand storytelling, senior employees are also dedicated to corporate storytelling, spreading the word about Nike's core values to outsiders, their distribution channel partners, and their own employees. The initiation of new employees at Nike starts with a two-day immersion in the Nike story. They hear about Nike's heritage of innovation. They hear the founding myth (the core element of any brand's story): Coach Bill Bowerman founded the company because he wanted his team to have better running shoes than anything then available. He knew that every ounce removed from a shoe's weight would relieve 200 cumulative pounds of burden from a runner during a one-mile race. Bowerman spent time in his workshop pouring rubber into the family waffle iron and created Nike's famous "waffle sole." Since then, Nike has been dedicated to providing athletes with superior-performing sports equipment, giving them the confidence to achieve their maximum capability.

Steven Pinker, in his book *How the Mind Works*, describes how dramatic scholar Georges Polti cataloged the number of plots in all of the world's fiction and drama. (And you think your job is tough!) He found that more than 80% of fictional stories are defined by adversaries, by tragedies involving kinship, or by tragedies involving love. (Copywriters, get moving!) This echoes our personal stories, which are also about rivalries, conflict, guilt, jealousy, and love.

Son retraces father's footsteps in Vietnam.

SON: Said, "You had to be there."

SON: Well, here I am.
(MUSIC: ...COMING.)

How you doing?

SON: No. I'm on leave. I'm in Vietnam.

FATHER: Vietnam?
SON: Yeah.
FATHER: Let's talk, son.

(MUSIC: AND IT APPEARED TO BE A LONG...)

Courtesy of AT&T. Reprinted with permission.

AT&T has fielded some of the most memorable advertising stories of the past decade. In one spot (created by Young & Rubicam), a mother is dropping her daughter off at college. Memories of her daughter as a child flash through her head, perfectly synchronized to Frank Sinatra's tune, "Our Love Is Here to Stay." The spot makes its point about AT&T calling card services in a memorable way because it taps into our emotions. Other AT&T ads have told of a son retracing his father's steps in Vietnam, a mother who cancels a business meeting to take her kids to the beach, and two teenagers who flirt innocently via computer.

Both large and small brands have stories to tell that consumers want to hear. A small Pittsburgh (Pennsylvania) savings and loan, Brentwood Savings Bank, had historically marketed CDs in the conventional way banks have marketed CDs for decades—by placing rate ads in local newspapers. But CDs became harder to sell when mutual fund alternatives could trumpet 30% annual gains. Newspaper ads were no longer working.

Brentwood Savings solved its problem by recognizing that sometimes people make decisions with their hearts even more than with their brains. The company switched from newspapers to TV, and each ad told a story, stoking the emotional connection between community customers and the bank.

One story related how in 1922 the bank's first employee collected deposits from mill workers in an orange crate and the next morning, used the same crate to carry back their receipts. Another story told how a loan from Brentwood helped a local dance instructor achieve her dream of owning a dance studio, thus enabling the community to train its own aspiring ballerinas. Storytelling has worked extremely well for Brentwood Savings. The bank reports a 38% gain in deposits in the two years the new campaign has run. Telling stories is a powerful ways to get attention.

Too many ads today abandon storytelling narrative in favor of beautiful execution and amazing special effects. Then, $1 million later, brand managers wonder why their ads, high on production values and low on narrative, aren't getting the degree of attention they should. In a schizophrenic media world of conflicting messages and overwhelming sensation, the art of storytelling is becoming more important, not less so.

# Sequenced Messaging

In the traditional marketing world (where persuasion physics reigns supreme), marketers tend to create stand-alone ads that don't necessarily refer to other ads or derive meaning from other ads. Ads are often so unrelated that account executives merely rotate them randomly into a predetermined media schedule—without much concern over the sequence.

When we think of advertising as a story to be told, we view the marketing communications plan and its message components quite differently. We begin to think more like publishers and less like conventional advertisers. We begin to think about how to publish our story. Each ad has meaning as part of a larger whole. The story can't be told out of sequence. The spacing, timing, and positioning of each message are critical. For example, on the web, cutting-edge ad-delivery technology now gives marketers the ability to manage the storyboarding of their ads by constructing ads in a series and then predefining their sequence of exposure regardless of which web site the user views.

Scott Bedbury, in charge of marketing at Starbucks, believes brands are a story that is never completely told. It's evolving all the time. "This connects with something very deep—a fundamental human appreciation of mythology. People have always needed to make sense of things at a higher level."

Tell prospects the story of your brand in an engaging, entertaining way. Ensure that all brand messages carry a piece of the narrative that will advance the story. Storytelling is a powerful tool of attention mechanics.

# 12

# Mingle

The currency of the New Economy won't be money, but attention.
*Michael H. Goldhaber, "Attention Shoppers," Wired,
December 1997*

If you want to get widespread attention in a crowded room, you're going to have to move around. It's a mistake to stay in one place all the time. Staying in one place puts significant constraints on the number of people you can connect with in a limited amount of time. You have to work the room. You have to move around, and when it comes to target audiences, in the words of attention mechanics, you have to *mingle*.

## Mingling among Target Audiences

The marketing communications industry has had a long-standing and growing fixation on targeting. It is an unquestioned axiom that if targeting is good, more targeting is better. The sharper our aim, the better. The more precisely we can pinpoint our key prospects, the better. The more effectively we can eliminate "wasted" impressions or ad exposures from the media plan, the better.

It's curious that targeting has achieved such a chauvinistic following in marketing and media circles, because targeting is not treated with such fetishlike devotion in many nonmarketing disciplines. People do not automatically equate targeting with efficiency or effectiveness in other areas. Targeting is considered merely one stratagem of efficiency. Here's an example.

In medicine, there are two main ways to treat cancer nonsurgically: radiation therapy (targeted) and chemotherapy (diffused, nontargeted). Radiation therapy is not always superior to chemotherapy by virtue of its targeting specificity. When the cancer is confined to a small area, radiation treatment aimed specifically at that spot may be indicated because it's the most efficient way to kill that type of cancer without killing the patient. However, for cancer that has spread throughout the body, chemotherapy (a diffuse, nontargeted method) may be more efficacious. Targeting, per se, is not critical.

Some are questioning the established dogma that targeting is good. (To paraphrase an old joke, it's time to let our karma run over our dogma.) Harvard business professor Clayton Christensen, author of *The Innovator's Dilemma*, suggests that old targeting rules of thumb can be deadly—in particular, the 80-20 rule that says you should target the 20% of customers who account for 80% of a typical company's sales volume. Followed blindly, this rule leads to continuing focus on a narrower and narrower band of customers until they completely marginalize the company. Any firm balanced so precariously on such a thin customer base is ripe for toppling.

One of the business world's most famous visionaries, Peter Drucker, has repeatedly voiced the same concern. Focusing exclusively on your own customers is the myopic road to ruin. Firms must constantly cultivate noncustomers and question why they are drawn to competitive brands—because in most brand categories, the majority of customers buy other brands sometimes or always.

> . . . noncustomers are as important as customers, if not more important: because they are potential customers. There are very few institutions . . . where noncustomers do not amount to at least 70% of the potential market. And yet very few institutions know anything about noncustomers—very few of them know . . . who they are. And even fewer know why they are not customers. Yet it is always with noncustomers that changes always start.
>
> The rapid decline of the American department store in the 1970s . . . was not caused by customers deserting them . . . but a new

breed of educated working woman did not adopt the department store habit. She didn't have the time. She was not a customer. The department stores paid little attention to her. By the time she became the biggest part of the affluent middle class, it was too late.[1]

Targeting current customers to the exclusion of noncustomers could be precisely the wrong strategy in many cases. In political elections, politicians do not aim their appeals exclusively at party loyalists. Successful politicians (those who actually win elections) know that it's just as important, perhaps even more so, to target "uncommitteds," the swing voters who can tip the balance.

Although targeting should not be equated to efficiency, it should not be confused with *addressing*, either. Addressing is *always* good, and I believe that people really have this in mind when they fixate on the inherent goodness of targeting.

All messages must be addressed to someone or some group. They can't be created any other way. The addressee, the intended receiver, must be a driving consideration during the creative process. But addressing and targeting are not the same. It's just as feasible to address an individual in a nontargeted way as it is to address a group in a targeted way.

Here's an example of the former. Consider the romantic sports fan who wants to propose to his intended in the most public, dramatic way possible. Pulling every string he can pull, he arranges for his proposal to stream across the Spectravision board in a packed football stadium just before halftime: MIRANDA, WILL YOU MARRY ME?

That message, blasted to 50,000 screaming fans, is addressed to one person, Miranda, albeit in a nontargeted way (i.e., everyone in the stadium is *targeted*, but only one person is *addressed*).

So attention mechanics does not confuse targeting with efficiency or with addressing. It views targeting as merely one technique for achieving efficiency—and not the only one.

## Spectrum Targeting

Another efficiency technique (opposite from targeting on the efficiency scale) is mingling, diffusion across targets, or what attention mechanics calls *spectrum targeting*. At my firm, we have experimented with this approach, and I sometimes talk about a box to explain it.

A traditional brand target audience definition is like a box. We define a target audience by putting metaphorical brackets around specific groups (defined demographically, psychographically, behaviorally, geographically, or in some combination of ways).

Take a simplistic target definition, such as "women aged 25 to 54." If this phrase is part of our target definition, the walls of the box are the age and sex constraints of the group. In effect, we are saying that, to our brand's franchise, each woman aged 25 to 54 has an importance value of 100%, and everyone not in the definition has an importance value of 0%.

On a graph, conventional target audience definitions look like a box: just one bar. Inside the box, the implied value is 100%; outside the box, the implied value is 0%. Traditional targeting divides people into just these two classes, target and nontarget. "There are two classes of people in the world," went Robert Benchley's famous remark, "those who divide the world into two classes and those who do not." Traditional targeters are among the former.

That's the traditional world of targeting. In the *real* world, by contrast, customer groupings are never so neat. In fact, for any conceivable product or service, everybody and anybody could be a customer. I might be a customer for a Boeing C-17 transport airplane that can carry tanks

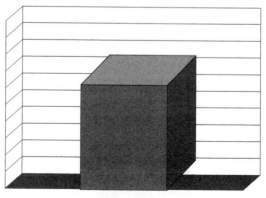

A traditional brand target audience is like a box.

**Target**

and troops into battle and land on some of the world's shortest runways—or I might not. General Colin Powell, when he was chairman of the Joint Chiefs of Staff, might have been a customer for such a plane as well. Although my probability of actually being a customer is extremely low, it is never, in fact, 0%. General Powell's probability of being a customer is far higher—perhaps 80 or 90%.

This is a silly example, but the point is fair. Customer groupings are not fixed quantities. They are constantly changing. New customers are dripping into the brand's bucket as lapsed customers leak out holes in the bottom. And for every customer in the bucket at a given moment in time, there is another, likely larger, group considering becoming customers. And behind that consideration set is another group that might be influencing them in some way—and so on and so on. In the real world, everyone has a probability between 0 and 100 percent of being a customer for any product or service, so our potential target audience cannot be narrowly defined in terms of a single box. Our graph would look more like a spectrum of bars, with each bar corresponding to the probability for each person in the population being a customer. (Histograms are the most useful types of charts for this exercise. Histograms array bars by height. Most histograms tend to show what looks like a bell curve—a hump of high-value bars in the middle and progressively shorter bars on either side.)

**Spectrum targeting is more like a bell curve of possibilities.**

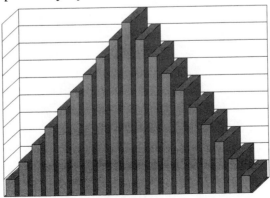

**Target**

We can use these sorts of tools to match the spectrum of media audiences to the spectrum of our brand's customer probabilities. Viewed this way, every ad impression has a value, too—somewhere between 0 and 100%. We can use the spectrum to examine the relative efficiency of different media schedules.

## The Targeting Uncertainty Principle

In Chapter 1, we discussed quantum mechanics as the inspiration for attention mechanics. In quantum mechanics, the Heisenberg uncertainty principle states that it is impossible to accurately measure both the position and momentum of a subatomic particle simultaneously. There is a sort of uncertainty principle for targeting as well. Given that targets have two dimensions, probability and time, an individual's probability of being a customer is never fixed at a certain value, but rather fluctuates between 0 and 100% over time. I just ate, so my customer probability for Kentucky Fried Chicken just dropped from 90% to 5%. Customer's target probabilities rise and fall over time. The more we try to fix a probability without respect to time, the higher the uncertainty.

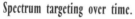

Spectrum targeting over time.

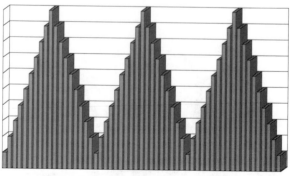

**Target**

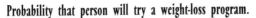

Probability that person will try a weight-loss program.

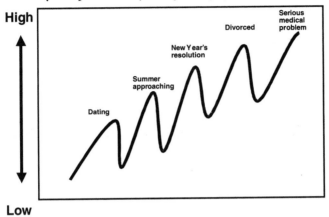

Take a look at how probabilities might rise and fall for a person considering a weight-loss program.

Taken together, these two concepts (defining targets by probabilities and taking into account how these probabilities change over time) are captured by what I call *spectrum targeting*. Spectrum targeting can be complex to execute, but the idea is simple. People pay more attention to messages when they're relevant.

# 13

# Network

**The attention economy makes creating and maintaining lasting engagement with consumers more critical than ever before.**
*Kevin Roberts, CEO, Saatchi & Saatchi London*

Mingling is one way to get attention in a crowded room. By moving around you increase your odds of finding someone *somewhere* who'll pay attention to you. But in the end, mingling, by itself, can be unsatisfying. Mingling is random, not purposeful. It doesn't aim at anything in particular. It doesn't move things forward.

Some people *do* have a goal in mind as they move through the room. To accomplish it, they absorb information in one spot, relay it in another, get introduced by one guest, then introduce that guest to a new group later on. They have moved beyond mere mingling to *networking*.

Minglers move around the target spectrum to get attention. Networkers move around the media spectrum, drawing connections as they go. From the vantage point of attention mechanics, networking is the most powerful strategy for getting and holding attention. Given networking's importance, I've devoted two chapters to it. Here in Chapter 13 I describe the three ways communications efforts can be networked to achieve significant gains in marketing performance: (1) across media, (2) across disciplines, and (3) by networked communications. In Chapter 14, I describe how to build a fully networked communications program for your brand.

# The Power of the Network: Metcalfe's Law

The power of the network has been often heralded by cyberscribes of the Internet age, but never so elegantly as by Bob Metcalfe. Metcalfe is the founder of 3Com and the inventor of Ethernet, the foundation technology for local area networks, to name just two accomplishments. Metcalfe is also famous for formulating Metcalfe's law, the idea that the value of a network increases dramatically with each additional node, or user. Metcalfe's law states that the value of a network is equal to the number of users squared. As the network grows larger, the greater the advantage of being connected to it.

For example, consider telephone network. A one-user telephone network is useless—you can't call anybody. But create a two-user telephone network, and the value isn't just twice as good as the single-user network, it's four times greater (two users squared). If our telephone network grows to 10 users, then the value of the network is geometrically greater still. It's not just 10 times better than the single-user network, it's 100 times better (10 users squared), because now all kinds of connections are enabled. Person 1 can talk to person 3. Person 7 can connect with person 9, and so on.

Scott McNealy, CEO of Sun Microsystems (and professional gadfly to the world's wealthiest human), has long promoted the potency of networks with his mantra, "The network is the computer." The capability of even the fastest isolated supercomputer pales in comparison to the power of a tightly connected computing network. Networks are more important than stand-alone computers. Networks can perform feats that individuals cannot.

The Internet itself is powerful by virtue of its being a network (a "network of networks"). This insight runs counter to what many marketing pundits say, because much of the marketing hype about the Internet misses the key point—it is not *interactivity*, but *connectedness* that makes the Internet potentially more powerful than all other media.

Most Internet marketing evangelists point to *interactivity*—the ability to engage in a two-way communication—as the defining feature of the Internet and the one functionality that best differentiates the new online medium from traditional offline media. Certainly, interactivity is an interesting feature, but the heart and soul of the Internet is the *connectedness* that it enables.

Attention mechanics views not just the Interent but the entire gamut of marketing communications as a potential network for your brand—what I call a *communications network*. From packaging to advertising, from TV to the web, attention mechanics puts the notion of a unified communications network front and center in the marketing architecture. In attention mechanics (to paraphrase McNealy), *the network is the ad*.

One reason networked communications are so powerful is that they mimic the way our brains work. Neurologists have discovered that mental processes such as speech, memory, vision, and so on, are not confined to one spot in the brain, but rather are distributed across different regions throughout the brain. In an analogous way, networked communications are distributed communications.

## Advantages to Marketing across a Network

There are numerous advantages to distributing your brand's messages throughout a communications network, over a network that is broader than a single medium, or even within a single marketing function.

### Relevance

A communications network offers your brand *multiple opportunities* to build brand image, engage in commerce, and build commitment and loyalty. Multiple opportunities translate to *more relevant interactions* with prospects. That increases the odds that prospects will be exposed to brand messages when and where they need the information.

### Navigation

A communications network is *interactive*. It functions to *steer prospects along the consideration path* toward commitment and loyalty. Prospects can travel the path at their own pace. A communications network enables customers to *navigate your brand*.

### Time

A communications network gives your brand *more time* to communicate to the depth required. It also allows your brand to blend a variety of message types—some brief, others long—but each appropriate to the time and place of customer engagement. And it allows the flexibility to deliver messages at the appropriate time, *in real time or anytime,* on demand.

### Route around Damage

A communications network reduces risk by *routing around damage.* For example, the Internet is designed to keep functioning even in the event a piece of it is under nuclear attack, but this attribute applies broadly to any network. If excessive zapping damages my TV campaign, then my public relations effort will still get through. If my web site goes down, my catalog and call center can pick up the slack and continue to function.

### Relevant Ubiquity

A communications network enables your brand to *seem ubiquitous* to prospects. Weaving the Internet into the brand's network extends that ubiquity through time (24-7) and space (global reach). In practice, no brand can be everywhere all the time, but a brand might strive for an ideal labeled *relevant ubiquity*—that is, seeming to be everywhere, but only when a prospect needs the information. To accomplish this, marketers need to first identify the times and places that a brand is most relevant to prospects, then spread messages there.

### Time and Space Flexibility

Communications networks offer brands flexibility in distributing messages through time and space. Here are some of the possible elements of a communications network, organized by time and place of contact with prospects:

|  | **Same Place** | **Different Place** |
| --- | --- | --- |
| **Same Time** | Face-to-face selling<br>Conferences<br>Conventions | Telephone<br>Online chat rooms<br>Instant messages<br>Videoconferencing<br>TV, radio |
| **Different Time** | Retail locations, kiosks<br>Out-of-home media<br>Vending machines | Internet, WWW<br>E-mail<br>Print media |

## Three Ways to Network

There are three levels of sophistication for distributing your brand's messages through a network: across media, across disciplines, and by fully networked communications.

The most basic way to network is to spread communications across multiple media, which increases the odds that your brand will intercept the right consumer at a relevant moment. A substantial body of research provides additional support for a multimedia approach. Communications are more powerful when more than one medium is used to get the message across.

Three ways to distribute brand messages.

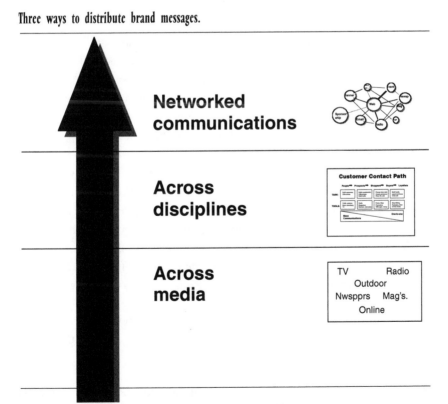

**Network strategy hierarchy**

## Network across Media

Most ad campaigns require more than one medium. That's a good thing, because a multimedia strategy is almost always more effective than a single-medium campaign. The sole exception is when a brand's budget is so small that creative production across two media is unaffordable.

Earlier, I discussed the baked-in biases that dominate so many brand categories. For example, packaged-goods products gravitate toward television (i.e., a bias for TV is baked into the category). Baked-in biases are bad. Even worse are media plans that employ only a single medium, putting all, or almost all, their eggs into one media basket—all TV for packaged-goods brand A, all print for appliance B, and so on.

Marketing consultant and media research pioneer Alvin Achenbaum has called advertisers' obsession with television commercials the "sixth sin of brand mismanagement":

> The sixth sin of brand mismanagement is the obsession with so-called advertising creativity and preoccupation with television: Taking a whack at marketers' and advertising agencies' obsession with creative execution is no doubt a form of heresy, but there is ample evidence, if marketers would only open their eyes to it, that creative executions do not have the leverage generally attributed to them. What makes this a serious problem is that the amount of money and time devoted to creative execution is way out of proportion to what can be achieved . . . hence, until we get some imaginative zero-based thinking into the media area, no amount of message creativity is going to make up for the tenfold decline in media productivity during the last twenty years. . . . *Marketers must readjust their marketing communications programs in order to restore the former power of marketing* [my emphasis]. . . . There is probably more leverage in media today than there is in so-called creativity.[1]

A brand should not rely on only a single medium to deliver its message. Supportive evidence for this point of view is mounting fast. In recent studies, my firm has found the following:

• With a fixed budget, two or more media build reach more quickly than single-medium plans.

- Multimedia plans are generally superior at contacting hard-to-reach segments.
- Media plans that use two or more media are generally superior to single-medium plans in balancing frequency of ad exposure across the population (minimizing needless repetition pileups).
- Multimedia campaigns are superior in accomplishing a variety of different communications tasks (for example, using TV to establish the brand's image in a highly visual or emotional manner combined with online media for intensive follow-through).
- And most important of all, multiple media often yield stronger communication effects than one medium alone. (Supportive studies have examined a broad spectrum of measures: brand imagery scores, claimed trial, key message playback, and a host of others.)

These new data streaming in from the research community are changing minds and influencing media strategists to move in new directions. It is becoming clearer that, given a fixed budget, a blend of different media will produce stronger communication than will only one medium. For example, Claritin (allergy medicine), in its fall 1999 campaign, used four different media to drive home its message: Television ads grabbed attention and directed people to an 800 number, a web site, and an issue of *Health* magazine to learn more.

## A Media Mix Delivers Stronger Communication

| Source | Method | Benefits of multiple media versus single medium |
|---|---|---|
| Magazine Publishers of America, "The Advertising Impact of Magazines in Conjunction with Television," 1990. | Copy test among 800 women | Brand imagery and preferences stronger |
| Examples of media synergies in Communicus studies, CCS LTD, 1993. | Panel survey | Claimed trial substantially stronger |
| "Media Synergy: The Danger of Putting All Your Message Eggs in One Media Basket," The PreTesting Company, 1991/1992. | Copy tests | Key message playback significantly stronger |

The move toward multimedia campaigns is a direct consequence of media proliferation. Instead of relying only on TV, only on print, or only on online advertising, it's more important than ever to find ways to *creatively blend a number of different media to accomplish a range of different tasks*. Multimedia campaigns have become a necessity in today's highly fractured media environment. Our media consumption habits have shattered into millions of different patterns. It is no longer safe to assume that we can reach most of our prospects with Thursday night's NBC lineup, a schedule in *People* magazine, or any other single media property. As with snowflakes, our personal media diets are unique.

In a report for *Brill's Content* magazine,[2] reporter Leslie Heilbrunn underscored the diversity among individual media consumption patterns in the United States by tracking 10 people's media diets for a single day in October 1999. Heilbrunn then matched each minute of media exposure to its source and calculated "mind-share" percentages by media owner. The results were surprising in their diversity and variety. For example, here are the mindshare percentages for each of the four 40-something adults:

## Daily Mind-Share Percentages

| Richard Kestenbaum | Brian Rhodes |
| --- | --- |
| 1. Disney 26% | 1. McGraw-Hill 33% |
| 2. *New York Times* 13% | 2. KEYN-FM 19% |
| 3. Yahoo! 12% | 3. Time Warner 10% |
| 4. C-Span 10% | 4. News Corp. 7% |
| 5. AM-FM radio 9% | 5. NBC 7% |
| 6. Time Warner 7% | 6. Other 24% |
| 7. Dow Jones 6% | |
| 8. Other 17% | |

| Heather Wilson | Allison O'Melia |
| --- | --- |
| 1. Journal Publishing 22% | 1. Clear Channel 28% |
| 2. National Journal Group 15% | 2. Citadel 21% |
| 3. News Communications 9% | 3. Bertelsmann 18% |
| 4. *Washington Post* 5% | 4. Post & Courier 15% |
| 5. *Congressional Quarterly* 5% | 5. Time Warner 8% |
| 6. Scripps 5% | 6. Other 10% |
| 7. C-Span 5% | |
| 8. Other 34% | |

Marketers who are serious about reaching us must be prepared to cast a wide multimedia net. But reach, by itself, is merely one benefit of a multimedia campaign. Brands that stage multimedia campaigns can also exploit the powerful advantages of complementary cross-media messaging. Brands can seduce consumers with one set of messages while inviting them to learn more in another medium in the campaign. Cross-media messaging is the start of a dialogue between the brand and the consumer.

Here's an example of using one medium as an invitation to learn more in another medium[3]:

> When interior design student Melissa Cohen decided the time was right to have a child, she acted fast. Cohen, who lives in NYC, was already 38 and statistically her fertility was decreasing at a rate of 2 percent each year. One day as she was searching for design information in the Web and watching TV, an advertisement for iVillage—the women's network—came on the tube. Cohen left her research project behind for the moment and typed in the iVillage URL. She navigated through the site until she found a page on fertility offering tons of information on ways to increase her likelihood to conceive. "It was great information that I really needed," says Cohen. "And even though I'd heard of iVillage before, I don't think I would have clicked on the site if the ad hadn't come on."

Networking across media is a powerful tool of attention mechanics. It recognizes that media properties will continue to multiply, and as they do, no single medium will be able to carry the burden of all the brand's communications goals. Brands will need to weave a tapestry of contacts with consumers, and they will need a variety of media to do it. No single medium will offer enough reach, enough frequency, enough touch. Only a multimedia presence will produce the desired effects. Only a multimedia plan can increase the odds that consumers will encounter the brand in a wide variety of relevant situations and contexts.

## Network across Disciplines

Another dimension to networking has to do with the diversity of communications disciplines employed by a brand. Does a brand use only PR, only advertising, or a variety of different techniques? To navigate successfully in an attention deficit society, marketers must expand the definition of advertising to include an entire range of new avenues.

Just as a multimedia approach is becoming more attractive within the discipline of advertising, a multidisciplinary approach is becoming more attractive within the field of marketing. The mantra among many forward-looking marketing chiefs today is "integrated marketing communications" (forward-looking marketing folk being, by nature, disinclined to choose ordinary, monosyllabic mantras). *Integrated marketing communications* refers to the process of coordinating messages across media and disciplines so that, wherever messages appear, they drive home the brand's singular selling proposition.

Marketers must become adept at deploying a blend of different communications. Charles Frenette, Coca-Cola's chief marketing officer, provides an instructive example:

> Advertising is just one component of our communication. If we need to reconnect every day, a billion times a day, we have to use all elements of the marketing mix. One could argue that it's probably 25% of the communication mix for us. Sponsorship, experiential marketing, grassroots activities, what we do inside the store to create theater for the brand, those are the things you will see evolving as we go forward.[4]

Integrated marketing shepherds customers along the shopping and buying path toward brand loyalty and on to advocacy, even evangelism. Great marketing plans orchestrate many disciplines, giving each an appropriate role in the process and coordinating messages along the way. The goal of almost every marketing plan is to push people who haven't been our customers to become prospects who might need our product to shoppers, buyers, and, finally, loyal repeat customers.

Seth Godin, author of *Permission Marketing*, cites the example of summer camp. Summer camps use magazine ads to prompt inquiries from interested parents. An ad's sole job is to get parents to request a brochure. The brochure's job is to prompt parents to request a meeting with a representative. The representative's job is to close the sale. The blend of communications works in unison to propel prospective customers forward through the customer contact path.

The marketing task for each stage of this path is different. For example, to convert people to prospects, the task might be to get attention and build awareness. But to convert buyers to loyalists, the task might be to build an interactive selling relationship.

Just as the tasks are different at each stage of the game, so, too, are the tools necessary to achieve them. For example, public relations and advertising might work best to attract attention, but direct marketing, packaging, or online communications might work best to build a selling relationship.

A particular communications tool might be appropriate at any stage of the process, but in general, the closer to the front of the path, the more important mass communications will be, and the closer to the end point on the path, the more important one-to-one communications will be. For most brands, the marketing opportunity is greater at one or two points in this process. Understanding that will help marketers focus on the right tools for the job.

In their book, *Channel Champions*, coauthors Evan Hirsh and Steven Wheeler cite museums as an example of a customer contact path. Having once visited their local museum, some people believe they have

Customer contact path tasks and tools.

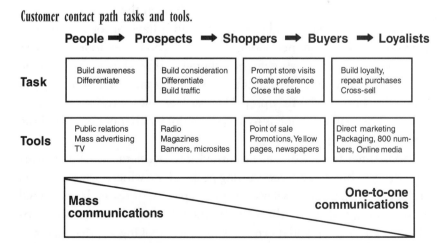

assuaged their civic duty. But the museum's job is to get you to return repeatedly. Museums do that in a variety of ways: by promoting school visits, by putting on new exhibitions, by involving people in archaeological digs, by taking exhibits on tour, and so on. "Greater interaction gives people the opportunity to become more and more involved. Experiencing the same product in different ways allows it to remain fresh."[5]

### Blockage and Acceleration Points

When mapping out the customer contact path, marketers should seek to identify blockage and acceleration points on which to focus the communications plan.

*Blockage points* are bottlenecks along the path where customers offer some resistance to moving forward. For example, blockage occurs when customers perceive a brand losing momentum. At that point, customers resist moving forward along the path. A brand may need news that will boost customers' perceptions of it.

Sometimes customers raise their hands but don't find an outlet for more information. Again, they're stuck along the path. A brand may need to provide in-depth information that's easier to access. Many other potential danger signs could indicate blockages in a brand's contact path: Consumers are not exposed to messages; consumers are exposed but don't notice; consumers notice but don't perceive differentiation and/or relevance. Communications plans need to clear the blockages and eliminate the bottlenecks to keep customers flowing through the system.

*Acceleration points* are places where brands have an opportunity to speed the flow of customers along the path. Periodic reminder messages can boost customers who might otherwise slow down and become attracted to a competitor's brand. Cross-selling and "selling up" ("you want fries with that?") may propel a customer toward the loyalty destination. The marketer's job is to keep the contact channel open and the customers flowing.

Sometimes blockages can be turned into accelerators. A few years ago, we were hired to do a consulting project for a winery, which wanted an independent point of view of its media plan. Our research uncovered a compelling fact about the wine business—most consumers are confused! We trudge up and down the wine aisle, looking at price tags, trying to find a label design that appeals to us. We desperately need information to help us distinguish one brand from another at the point of purchase. Our client's original media plan had not focused much attention on this problem; rather, TV ads were designed exclusively to build general awareness of the client's product. We recommended that some funds be redeployed to clear this communications blockage and create an acceleration opportunity instead. The program consisted of a variety of in-store media and packaging enhancements.

### Benefit of Networking Across Disciplines

Networking across disciplines is a way to reunite the seemingly separate worlds of public relations, advertising, sales promotion, direct marketing, and so on. Not so long ago, all of these disciplines were one. But over the past 80 years, we have witnessed them splinter into separate specialties. Advertising deals with building the brand and creating awareness and image. Direct marketing builds loyalty and introduces selling efficiencies. Sales promotion incentivizes both the consumer and the trade to stock up.

The trend toward specialization continues: When a field within marketing communications attains sufficient sophistication (and gets a

Customer contact path blockage and acceleration points.

**People ➡ Prospects ➡ Shoppers ➡ Buyers ➡ Loyalists**

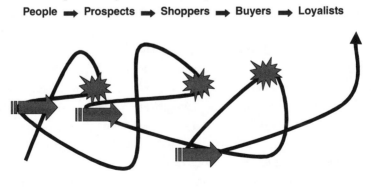

 **Blockage**     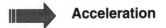 **Acceleration**

client or two!), it branches off from its parent discipline. Public relations branched off in the 1920s and 1930s. Direct marketing splintered off in the 1970s and 1980s. Currently, the emergence of *customer relationship management* as a discipline separate from its parent, *direct marketing,* seems imminent.

Clearly, the expertise of specialists is desirable. But this expertise has come at the expense of integrated communications. Marketing specialties have become so compartmentalized, it is as if we are forcing consumers to jump from the "advertising boulder" to the "direct boulder" to the "sales promotion boulder" to follow our consideration path across the stream.

Brands need communications plans that flow seamlessly across marketing disciplines, plans that minimize the artificial boundaries that have grown up around marketing disciplines. The situation is similar to the one facing patients in our medical system today. Medical science has spawned specialties, subspecialties, and specialties within subspecialties. Patients benefit from this compartmentalized expertise, of course, but they also yearn for the general practitioner who will manage their care holistically to counterbalance the specialist who treats each ailment mechanically. Marketing doctors need to treat their patients (i.e., brands) holistically, too.

That's what attention mechanics aims to do. Through strategies such as networking across disciplines, attention mechanics addresses the need to reunite the separate and various skills of modern marketing communications.

Most established advertising agencies have been slow to engineer this desired marketing reunification. The prevailing financial management structure has been one stumbling block. By and large, marketing specialties within the largest ad agencies are managed as separate lines of business with separate profit and loss responsibility to the agency's corporate parent. This creates a financial disincentive for networking across disciplines, since each line of business sees its best interest as corralling as much of the marketing budget as possible so its income is maximized (at the expense of the other business units, of course).

My firm, Young & Rubicam, is different from most. Young & Rubicam has launched a variety of bold initiatives to repair the breach among marketing disciplines. One is called Y&R 2.1, a new global ad agency launched by Young & Rubicam in the fall of 1999. Its goal is to unleash the full meaning inherent in a brand and to do so across all communications channels. It aims to reintegrate all online and offline marketing services by eliminating the artificial boundaries between them. Specialists from every marketing field have been recruited to unite under the Y&R 2.1 umbrella. Y&R 2.1 is a reinvention of the ad agency model for the era of attention mechanics.

## Networked Communications

The most sophisticated form of networking—and the most powerful technique of attention mechanics—is *networked communications*. Networked communications means linking messages within media, across media, and across disciplines. Brands that connect every component of their campaign into a unified, rational system will see their marketing power multiplied many times.

By networking a brand's marketing messages together, we make it easier for people to form a rich network of memories associated with that brand. Networked communications facilitates branding. Why? Because brands are also networks.

At its most basic level, a brand is just a network of mental associations that exist in people's minds. Some of these associations include what we typically think of as a brand—logos, symbols, slogans, packaging, signage, and so on. But we tend to associate all sorts of other things with brands in our minds as well—your last experience using the brand, how easy or hard it was to find the brand in the store, what the salesclerk said about the brand, a joke told by a celebrity on a talk show that mentioned the brand, a recipe you found at the brand's web site, what your brother-in-law thinks of the brand, and so on.

Brands *are* networks, so marketing plans that include networklike features will build stronger brands.

### The Building-Block Past

Decades ago, some brands could rely on a few isolated ads, primarily in a single medium, to accomplish all of their marketing goals—from awareness through loyalty. Campaign strategists of that era left a legacy in their approach to campaign building, typically called the *building-block approach*.

The idea was that campaigns should be constructed of media building blocks, with *efficiency* first and *reach potential* second until the budget ran out. For many packaged-goods brands, that meant building a media plan starting with the most efficient building block, daytime TV, followed by the prime-time TV building block for reach, and then, if dollars remained, perhaps something exotic such as magazines or radio.

### The Networked Present . . . and Future

Today's marketing strategist must blend many messages and disciplines together to accomplish the same effect. Each message and each discipline plays a partial role in the process, but none stands alone. It is the combination that is effective, not the isolated pieces.

*Targeting* is really the wrong term to describe the dynamic marketing plans we are trying to create. A better term might be *funneling*. Peter Rip, general manager of web site Infoseek, observes that "the challenge for most marketing plans is to funnel a broad enough prospect base through a series of steps to transform them into loyal customers, not just to find a few immediate purchasers."[6]

The old building-block approach.

**Magazines**

**Prime-time TV**

**Daytime TV**

Carrying this thinking forward into the future, brands will find ways to snare customers with attention-grabbing messages and then recycle those customers throughout the entire mix of communications—increasing loyalty and deepening the relationship at each turn. Attention will serve as a sort of funnel that sweeps a wide path through the marketing landscape, scooping up prospects into the message recycling system.

Highly linked, networked messaging will lead to marketing communications programs that are not just integrated, but aggressively self-referential. Currently, most ad campaigns and communications programs are made up of discrete, stand-alone messages. In the future, ads and marketing communications of all forms will link to other campaign messages across all media platforms in a sort of continuous cross-referencing loop.

Jesse Bert, at ZDNet, calls this "spiral marketing" and "media weaving." Jim Nail, at Forrester, calls it "synchronized advertising." Seth Godin, at Yahoo!, calls it "fusion marketing." These and other forward-looking thinkers are abuzz about this idea, which Godin explains this way:

**The network is the ad.**

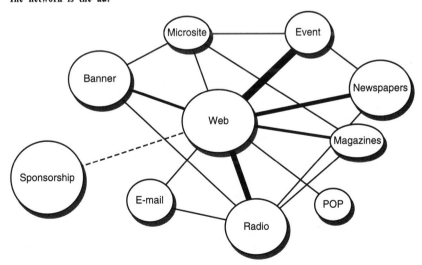

After the initial contact, after the first touch, you need a plan to take the prospect on a journey. Smart marketers lay out a suite of messages that make it easier to turn a stranger into a friend and a friend into a customer . . . [to be successful] a wide footprint is the all important first step . . . take a look at the folks who are winning online. Almost every one of them has made the big investment in a widespread media footprint that touches millions of potential customers.[7]

We stand at the very primitive beginnings of the development of networked communications. New and sophisticated ways of directing people throughout the message mix will have to be conceived and invented.

# 14

# Building a Networked Communications Plan

> We are shifting from a retail economy to what I call an attention economy.
>
> *Joe Kraus, cofounder of Excite*

The essence of a networked communications plan is *linking*. By linking and weaving our marketing messages together, we can create a messaging system far more powerful than any mere ad ever could be. In the future, a large part of our success or failure as marketers will depend on how effectively we respond to this challenge. In this chapter I focus on four guidelines for developing powerful networked plans: (1) Create links; (2) point to the web; (3) think navigation; and (4) exploit media network brands.

## Create Links

At my firm, we are now experimenting with various methods for linking communications. One simple method of linking messages is to list web sites and telephone numbers in offline media ads (TV, print, outdoor, radio). Or use online banner ads that link to your web site. Or embed TV-to-web links on interactive TV platforms such as WebTV.

Linkages need not be confined to the offline-to-online direction. Marketing messages can be connected in any combination of ways. Radio spots can guide consumers to this morning's newspaper ad for more information. E-mail messages can invite key customers to watch the debut of the new TV campaign on *ER* tomorrow night. Point-of-purchase displays can offer a toll-free number, and so on.

We classify links as *indirect* voice or text referrals or *direct* technology-enabled point-click referrals. Showing a web site address on a print ad is an example of an indirect link. Inserting a click-to-the-web link on interactive TV platforms such as webtv or DigitalConvergence.com is an example of a direct link. DigitalConvergence.com, which launched in the spring of 2000, will connect TV programming or ads directly to web content.

Another example of direct linking technology is Tranz-Send's MediaMan device, introduced at the January 2000 Consumer Electronics Show, which aims to link outdoor signs with web content. MediaMan is a handheld device that will enable passersby to interact with outdoor signs. Red dots on billboards or posters let people know that an ad is MediaMan-enabled. When a person sees the dot and presses a button on the device, it identifies which ad the user has pointed to, wirelessly retrieves further data from the company's web site, and transmits it back to the device.

Another firm, Xenote, is developing a type of real-world bookmarking technology to enable indirect links between TV or radio content and information on the web. A San Mateo, California, company, Xenote is developing a key-chain-sized device, the iTag, which will enable users to push a button to record the precise time a TV or radio spot piqued their interest. Later, uploaded tags from the iTag, by zeroing in on the content of that moment, allow the user to learn more. For example, users could retrieve information on the names of songs they'd heard, then link to online CD sellers to make a purchase.

Our link taxonomy also include "teaser" links to arouse curiosity, "learn more" links for customers who want more information, "notification" links to guide consumers to messages of potential interest, and "invitation" links that offer special information tailored to particular customers.

Linked messages were the centerpiece of our recent campaign for Adobe, the leading maker of graphics software, whose products are versatile and fun to use. Adobe knew that it could entice customers by getting them to try the software. We created a multimedia campaign to do just that.

Print, billboard, and online banner ads (e.g., www.defytherules.com) were graphically sophisticated and visually intriguing to grab attention. In addition, each ad was linked to a microsite on the web (basically, a customized section of Adobe's marketing web site). Links were both indirect (for print and outdoor billboards) and direct (for banner ads). When prospects followed the link, they found Adobe graphics software modules they could activate immediately (e.g., Adobe Photoshop 5.5 and Adobe Premiere 5.1). Inspiration became reality on demand.

Nike is another example of a network communications pioneer. In January 2000, Nike launched an innovative ad campaign that exploited the power of networked media. A series of television commercials were linked to microsites on the web. In one spot, sprinter Marion Jones challenges viewers to a race. The camera, as the viewer's proxy, tries to keep up with Jones as she weaves through streets and alleyways. The chase reaches a climax when the viewer accidentally bumps into a man who is juggling chain saws. As one saw is about to crash into the viewer's face, the screen freezes and a teaser link appears: "Continued at whatever.nike.com." At the microsite, viewers can choose alternative endings, access streamed versions of other spots in the campaign, and, of course, buy Nike shoes. "This is a hint of what's coming in the future," says Steve Sandoz, Wieden & Kennedy's interactive creative director.[1] He's right. Networked communications can turn a single 30-second TV spot into a 30-minute entertainment and shopping experience.

Brand marketers should begin linking their communications *now*. The first stage is easy: Indirect voice or text referral linkages should be woven into every component of the marketing plan—from ads to promotions to packaging. The second stage, direct technology-enabled linking, is harder, but marketers should begin experimenting with direct digital linkages as soon as possible.

The Internet is clearly the model here. Linking is part of its DNA. Extending linkages throughout and across all media forms is the chal-

"Adobe® software lets you do the impossible on the Web. Go see for yourself."

Adobe and the Adobe logo are trademarks of Adobe Systems Incorporated. Photograph by Glen Wexler. Reprinted with permission.

Adobe® is an expert at linking online and offline media.

Adobe and the Adobe logo are trademarks of Adobe Systems Incorporated. Photograph by Glen Wexler. Reprinted with permission.

lenge ahead. Promising advances seem to appear daily—webtv, Replay TV, Tivo, Wink, Command Audio, to name just a handful.

The Gap (clothing retailer) is an astute practitioner of web-centric, linked messaging. It promotes its web site at cash registers and in window displays in its stores. In some stores, The Gap has hooked up computer terminals for easy access to its web site. Items purchased online can be returned in stores, and vice versa.

Keith Wardell, CEO of Shop2U.com, offers the following linking tips to "clicks-and-mortar" marketers:

- Advertise your web site on mailings and in stores.
- Take requests for print catalogs through the web, by e-mail, or at retail sites.
- Make sure e-mails link back to specific web pages promoting that product.
- When a purchase is made through any channel, send an e-mail offer for a related product.
- Request e-mail addresses on customer service cards.
- Use e-mail to generate traffic to web or store events.
- Use e-mail to notify customers of order status, regardless of channel shopped.
- Use the web site to promote retail events.
- Present coupons on the web site—redeemable in stores or online.

## Point to the Web

The next step is to create a communications solar system with a web site sun radiating the complete story of the brand's proposition and other, lower-bandwidth media orbiting around it. (Credit for this idea goes to Mike Samet, media director of Young & Rubicam in the mid-1990s.) Each medium carries a piece of the brand's story—the piece that that medium can tell best.

All of the media function to draw prospects deeper into the messaging solar system. The web site sun provides the gravity that holds the entire system together. The messages orbiting at the outer edge of the system are entry portals. Their job is to serve as hooks to get a prospect's attention—and to make it easy for him or her to enter the company's orbit. The media link to each other, but also point to the web site sun at the center, where the brand can tell its story to its full depth—including every aspect of its selling, service, and relationship elements.

For example, IBM has received plaudits for its current e-business campaign—a seemingly ubiquitous message that IBM stands for electronic business. The campaign started with multipage ads in the *Wall Street Journal,* which sent people to IBM's web site. The print ads were accompanied by TV commercials, also directing prospects to the web site. Following the TV commercials, ads in trade publications and direct mail packages targeted key decision makers and, again, directed prospects to the web. Only the web site offered an actual selling message. All of IBM's ads in traditional media had been aimed at arousing curiousity and motivating consideration. The web site started the sale.

Many retailers are quick to adapt their business models to exploit the power inherent in this web-centric, clicks-and-mortar world:

- Barnes & Noble enables customers to order merchandise on its web site and have it delivered within two hours. George Colony, president of Forrester, labels this attention deficit marketing at its best.

Communications solar system.

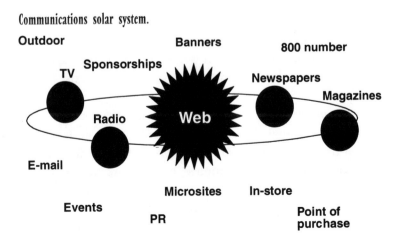

- Williams-Sonoma has integrated its in-store and online gift registries. Brides can log on and see what friends and relatives are buying for them in real time.
- Sears and Target shoppers can secure store credit cards instantly, just by visiting the stores' respective web sites.
- Banana Republic stores experimented with web stations that customers used to browse and order merchandise not carried in that store location.
- On the FAO Schwarz web site, shoppers can access a live web-cam view of store boutiques. If they see something they like, they can order it instantly.

These trailblazers are doing today what will become standard business practice tomorrow. They are synchronizing online and offline pricing and promotions. They are promoting their web sites in the stores and stores in their web sites. They are coordinating online and offline merchandising so the web site has the look and feel of the actual store. They are enabling ultimate flexibility by allowing customers to order online and pick up, return, or exchange merchandise at the retail store nearest them.

# Think Navigation

When creating a networked communications program for your brand, the biggest issues are not about persuasion—they are about navigation. A networked communications plan is designed to help prospects navigate your brand, and the model for this process already exists: the marketing web site.

Creating web sites is challenging because they are complex communications systems, not collections of isolated, stand-alone, messages. They fly in the face of every rule of thumb we learned in Advertising 101: Good ads should be single-minded, but web sites are multiminded. Good ads should aim at one target audience, but web sites are equally available to all possible target audiences.

*Advertising* is too narrow a term to describe marketing web sites, which are not ads, but multifaceted communications systems. They are complex pieces of information architecture. My colleague, Mike Samet, has said that creating a web site is the most daunting marketing challenge an advertiser could face. The process of developing the web site forces the advertiser to think through all of the brand's strategic navigational issues across all possible target audiences and across every step of the consideration path.

Samet and I used to talk about web site navigational issues in terms of urban planning. Web sites, we figured, are like cities. Navigating around cities and navigating around web sites are analogous. In the mid-1990s, we created a how-to guide for building great web sites, which was modeled on *The Death and Life of Great American Cities* by Jane Jacobs—the most influential single book in the history of town planning. From Jacobs we learned the importance of getting around easily, of avoiding dead ends, of creating frequent opportunities to turn a corner, of interweaving paths.

It may be instructive to think of networked communications plans as, in effect, giant web sites that extend beyond the Internet into offline media forms, retail locations, packaging, and even personal selling. As with web sites, networked communications plans must guide prospects fluidly along the consideration path. Individual message nodes must always lead somewhere else. There must be no dead ends.

When viewed this way, the artificial distinctions among marketing disciplines fall away. Ads, direct response programs, public relations—all blend seamlessly together into one synchronized information architecture. There is no ad. "Advertising must lose its obsession with ads."[2]

"It's very simple," concurs Phil Guarascio, GM's VP of marketing, "the line between sales promotions, event marketing, one-to-one, all those lines are blurred. So all those lines are falling down and it's one big budget."[3] *The network is the ad.*

## Exploit Media Network Brands

Traditional media owners are dealing with the same kinds of issues, and responding with the same sorts of answers. In fact, media owners are in the vanguard when it comes to linking their properties. MTV is launching a new game show called *Web Riot* that will link cable channel viewers to related content on a companion web site. ESPN and ABC promote "enhanced viewing" with tightly synchronized TV and online content during college and pro football games, with the web site offering team statistics, graphic displays of game information, trivia contests, and an interactive play-calling game. Advertisers are offered the opportunity to run banner ads that synchronize with TV ads.

Distribution is becoming less important in media branding. The media world is segregating rapidly into *conventional brands*, whose identities are intertwined with their distribution channel, and *network brands*, which cross boundaries and span distribution channels.

Let's take a look at where the media are headed.

1.  *Media brand identities will become unlinked with their distribution channels.* Historically, a media vehicle's brand identity was all bound up with its distribution channel. NBC was a network. *Newsweek* was a magazine. Now, however, media brand identities have to mean something apart from the distribution channel. When we think of ESPN five years from now, will that mean a cable channel? A web site? A magazine? Will it even matter?

2.  *Strong media brands, network brands, will more commonly extend across platforms and channels of distribution.* New kinds of media brands, dubbed *network brands*, are emerging. A media network brand has two characteristics:

- Focused content
- Multiple distribution platforms

Media network brand identities have meaning apart from their distribution platforms. Indeed, one hallmark of a media network brand is that its core brand proposition stays tightly focused even though the brand extends across multiple platforms. ESPN means "sports fan." Nickelodeon means "looking at the world from the kids' point-of-view" no matter what the channel.

3.  *Shared media content and linked marketing communications will become more common, almost expected.* Currently, most ad campaigns and communications programs are made up of discrete, stand-alone messages. Most media "brands" are really distribution channels in disguise. In the future, media content as well as ads will extend across all available

ESPN means "huge sports fan" whatever the medium.

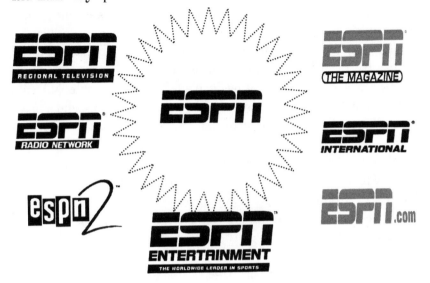

platforms, evolving into mininetworks that cross-promote and self-refer through all media platforms. And media owners will encourage network brand ingredients to be shared across all media platforms. For example, the network brand ESPN's popular *Sportscenter* show (an ingredient in its overall network brand) will extend from cable to the web to radio and into magazines.

4.  *Media companies will reshuffle staff across divisional lines to establish multiplatform network brand editors and publishers.* Current organizational structures rooted in "management by distribution channel" will give way to new structures organized around media network brands. *TV Guide* is a growing media network brand with a rapidly proliferating media stable that includes a weekly magazine, a web site, a cable channel, and an electronic program guide for digital TV. One day soon, AT&T and Murdoch's News Corporation (joint owners of the network brand), may decide to establish a single *TV Guide* brand manager, assisted by a single editor in charge of the content across all the platforms and a single publisher in charge of selling ads across all the platforms.

5.  *Network brands will revive cross-media deals in the form of network brand sponsorships.* In the early 1990s, much-touted ad-sales synergies

failed to materialize following the wave of giant media company mergers of the era. Media network brands may change that. Cross-media packaging, in the form of network brand sponsorships and marketing alliances, will be revived. Brands that choose media network partners with highly compatible and relevant content will be particularly effective in addressing receptive audiences across media platforms. For example, Nike and ESPN are both huge sports fans—in TV, web, radio, stores, and a magazine. IBM and the *Wall Street Journal* signify business—in the newspaper, online, and on the radio.

Network brand sponsorships may emerge as highly effective components of an attention mechanics strategy. To take advantage of network brand sponsorships, ad agencies will have to become more nimble. David Verklin, CEO of Carat North America, describes his experience at Hal Riney & Partners:[4]

> Now I want to talk about multiplatform deals. Many of you know that I ran a full service advertising agency until 18 months ago, and I'll tell you a dirty secret: It's that the creative side of the business hasn't been structured for joint media deals. You come to me at Hal Riney with a joint media deal that's got outdoor billboards, magazine campaigns, a one-third page black & white promotion, some fashion shows, some banners, and I go to the creative department and tell them I need some outdoor creative, I need a third page black & white, I need some internet stuff—I couldn't get a third page out of Hal Riney with a shotgun!

[Following the advice of my publisher, I want to make clear that Verklin never really threatened Hal Riney—with or without a shotgun—he was speaking metaphorically.]

# From Narrowband to Broadband Communications

There is an interesting parallel between computing technology and communications technology. In the computing field, growth went into hyperdrive when stand-alone computer boxes were linked together (first via LANs, then WANs, and now the Internet). When computers were linked together into networks, really interesting stuff started to happen.

We are now approaching a similar era of "networked" marketing communications. As with computers, once we link our marketing messages, really interesting stuff is bound to happen.

Internet distribution offers another instructive parallel. Currently, most people have narrowband access to the Internet. Narrowband means slow, typically dial-up, service. Downloading large files and complex images, much less video, takes forever. However, some telephone and media giants are now introducing broadband access to the Internet via cable modems and digital subscriber telephone lines. Broadband offers much faster (and always-on) service, providing a significantly more satisfying experience.

Networked, integrated marketing communications equate to broadband marketing. The quantum leap from persuasion physics to attention mechanics is like jumping from narrowband to broadband communications. Networking, which aims to integrate a multiplicity of messages into a unique and unified brand presence, is destined to become the most powerful strategy of attention mechanics.

# PART III

# Attention Mechanics: How to Get Started

# 15

# The Tools of Attention Mechanics

**Marketing is a contest for people's attention.**
*Seth Godin*, Fast Company, *April 1998*

Taken together, all of the strategies for getting attention in a crowded room form the outline of attention mechanics: Enter. Interrupt politely. Be introduced. Yell occasionally. Whisper. Find a quiet place. Be different. Mingle. Network. Be brief. Touch. Tell a story. Pay for it.

The marketplace is growing increasingly crowded and noisy, so marketers must respond by becoming increasingly clever at getting their brands noticed. In the short term, the most obvious ways to get attention are to interrupt the consumer and outshout the competition. But these easy solutions are becoming less effective over time. Shouting works well when everyone else is speaking normally. But when everyone else is shouting, only screaming will do.

The easy ways to get attention are the least conducive to the long-term health of the attention ecology. Intruding, shouting, and screaming are the least creative and least thoughtful (not to mention expensive) means to get a brand noticed. Continuing on this path will only lead to further declines in marketing's return on investment.

Attention mechanics represents a new approach to the planning and execution of marketing communications. Attention mechanics treats attention as a precious human commodity that must be respected and conserved. Attention mechanics as an approach to marketing communications represents a synthesis of push and pull marketing. It offers new techniques to guide marketing communications planning (e.g., momentum marketing, windows of opportunity, POP, spectrum targeting, linked messaging, and network brand sponsorships). Marketing is a contest for people's attention, and marketers need attention mechanics now more than ever.

To return to the two main goals stated in the book's Introduction, attention mechanics aims to (1) restore the power of marketing communications and (2) conserve that power for future generations. Accordingly, our overview of potential attention-getting strategies will array them along the axes defined by these two goals.

The vertical axis represents the impact of each strategem on media and marketing ecosystems over the long term. Strategies toward the top are more beneficial; they tend to preserve the ecosystem. Strategies toward the bottom are damaging; they tend to destroy the ecosystem. The horizontal axis represents the attention-generating power of the strategem. Strategies to the left are effective in getting attention. Strategies on the right are effective in both getting *and* holding attention. The accompanying graphic shows how attention mechanics positions each strategem on the matrix.

Attention mechanics points brand marketers to the strategies occupying the top half of the matrix. This domain of attention mechanics includes the kinds of strategies that will conserve the effectiveness of marketing communications for the future: Whisper. Be different. Find a quieter place. Touch. Tell a story.

Of all of the environmentally friendly strategies, the one in the upper right quadrant is the best of all: *Network*. This strategy is the most likely to be effective in both getting and holding attention. Brands need to network across media and across marketing disciplines. Marketers must become architects of networked communications.

Connect all brand messages together by linking them into a tightly interlocked message network. View every message node as an entry portal that will pull prospects into the network and advance them forward along the consideration path toward the web sun at the center. Provide customers with the navigational cues they need to follow the path. Networked communication is the most powerful strategy of attention mechanics.

| | Get Attention | Hold Attention | |
|---|---|---|---|
| Preserve attention ecosystem | • Mingle<br>• Tell a story<br>• Touch<br>• Be different<br>• Find a quieter place<br>• Whisper<br>• Yell occasionally<br>• Be brief<br>• Be introduced<br>• Pay for it<br>• Interrupt politely<br>• Grand entrance<br>• Enter | • Network | Attention mechanics |
| Destroy attention ecosystem | • Scream<br>• Offend<br>• Insult<br>• Intrude<br>• Repeat<br>• Shock | • Imprison<br>• Capture | Persuasion physics |

Attention is not the only criterion for successful communications, but attention is the first rung on the ladder, and brands can't skip over it if they intend to climb higher.

## Attention Mechanics: The Tools

Attention mechanics offers communications planners a new approach—neither push nor pull marketing, but a synthesis of both. Attention mechanics also offers communications planners a new tool set, shown in the accompanying graphic.

| Strategy | Tools |
|---|---|
| • Enter | • Momentum marketing |
| | • More ads |
| • Interrupt (politely) | • Relevant media content adjacency |
| | • Recency approach |
| • Be introduced | • Public relations |
| | • Celebrity / showcase environments |
| • Yell (occasionally) | • Balance yelling / continuity |
| | • Flexible planning (ongoing feedback and adjustments) |
| • Whisper | • Minimalist ad content |
| | • Curiosity-arousing street theater |
| | • Viral marketing |
| • Find a quieter place | • Deal with clutter |
| | • Avoid baked-in bias |
| | • Seek windows of opportunity |
| • Be different | • Differentiated brand proposition |
| | • POP |
| • Mingle | • Spectrum targeting |
| • Network | • Multimedia plans |
| | • Multidisciplinary plans |
| | • Linked messages |
| | • Customer contact path |
| | • Communications solar system |
| | • Media network brands sponsorship |
| • Be brief | • Balance hand-raiser with deep messages |
| | • Scale message to medium |
| • Touch | • Personal contacts |
| | • Online chat, live help |
| • Tell a story | • Sequenced messages |
| • Pay for it | • Online incentive programs |

To start down the road toward attention mechanics, brand marketers need not adopt all of these tools. But you should begin auditing your communications processes now. One way to assess priorities is to evaluate each tool of attention mechanics relative to its potential business gain versus cost of execution for your brand.

### Setting Priorities: Business Gain versus Cost

| | | Cost | |
|---|---|---|---|
| | | High | Low |
| Potential Business Gain | Large | Consider now | Do now |
| | Small | Do later | Consider now |

Brands can enjoy quick victories with inexpensive tools that will likely deliver a large or immediate business gain—tools such as *linking messaging* (to obliterate dead ends and ensure that every ad leads somewhere) and *mapping customer contact paths* (to make certain that marketing pressure is being applied where it will do the most good). Marketers should do these now.

# Comparing Attention Mechanics to Persuasion Physics

In Chapter 1, I described the concept of *persuasion physics*, the conventional wisdom in marketing circles. The graphic on page 174 shows how *attention mechanics* compares to persuasion physics in some key dimensions.

Persuasion physics delivers a rigid plan on a fixed annual planning cycle. Attention mechanics has a flexible planning horizon and expects ongoing changes and adjustments. It strives for *balance* between the need to yell and the need to talk normally. It especially seeks out windows of opportunity—times or places when and where competitive noise is light but sales potential is strong.

Persuasion physics produces highly polished stand-alone ad messages. Attention mechanics is more akin to publishing. Messages have meaning based on their sequence and relationship to other messages. There is a story to be told.

Persuasion physics succumbs to the baked-in bias in the marketer's category and focuses spending exclusively or primarily in a single medium. As additional budgetary resources become available, practitioners use the building-block method to add media components. Conversely, attention mechanics uses an integrated, multimedia approach

| | Persuasion Physics | Attention Mechanics |
|---|---|---|
| Planning horizon | • Rigid annual plan | • Flexible plan<br>• Ongoing changes<br>• Windows of opportunity |
| Campaign paradigm | • Standalone messages | • Publishing an ongoing story |
| Campaign architecture | • Single or primary medium<br>• Building block approach | • Integrated, multimedia<br>• POP<br>• Momentum marketing |
| Media role | • Mail carrier | • Lobbyist<br>• Network brand sponsorships |
| Target audience | • In a box | • Spectrum |
| Number of messages | • Fewer | • More |
| Creative integration | • Rotated ads | • Linked messaging |
| Measurement | • Upfront | • Downstream |

designed around a *primary organizing principle* (POP). It uses momentum marketing to manufacture news in a systematic way.

Persuasion physics views a medium as a mail carrier—good only for delivering the message. Attention mechanics views media as potential lobbyists for the brand. Network brand media sponsorships resonate with the brand's selling proposition.

Persuasion physics defines a target audience in a yes/no box. Attention mechanics apportions media weight relative to target probabilities.

Persuasion physics runs only a handful of ads repetitively. Attention mechanics demands that a far greater variety of ads be produced and run.

## Campaign Performance Based on Variations in Message and Medium*

| | | Message | |
| --- | --- | --- | --- |
| | | Lowest = 1 | Highest = 10 |
| Medium | Highest = 10 | 10 | 100 |
| | Lowest = 1 | 1 | 10 |

*A strong message in a strong medium is 10 times more effective than the same message in a weaker medium.

Persuasion physics rotates ads through individual media purchases. Attention mechanics uses linked, interlocking messages to cycle prospects through a continuous-loop communications system—advancing the buying process through the stages of awareness, consideration, purchase, and repeat.

Persuasion physics optimizes primarily one dimension of the marketing communications plan—the message dimension—within a largely fixed and repeating media strategy. Attention mechanics optimizes *both* dimensions—message and medium—which multiplies its power geometrically.

Decades of direct marketing experience show that an identical message performs differently given different media placements. A weak message in a strong, relevant medium can be 10 times more effective than the same message in a nonrelevant medium. But a strong message in a strong medium is not just 10 times more effective, it's 100 times more effective.

Persuasion physics puts the measurement emphasis up front in the campaign. Attention mechanics pushes the measurement emphasis downstream.

Attention mechanics points the way to a long list of new tools and techniques that advertisers can use to ignite the marketing process. The marketers' job is to identify appropriate techniques for a particular brand's situation. But marketers can do some simple things to get started *today:*

## Attention Mechanics: To-Do Starter Checklist

✓ Use more than one ad medium.
✓ Map out your brand's customer contact path.

✓ Identify the blockages and clear them.
✓ Identify the acceleration points—put the emphasis there.
✓ Alternate periodic marketing bursts with longer maintenance cycles.
✓ Make sure every message leads somewhere—no dead ends!
✓ Start experimenting with new ways to link ads together across media.
✓ Start a measurement program.

# 16

# Measurement

> Individuals need to realize there's a war going on between the market and consumers. It's a war for attention and time. The scarce resource is time.
>
> *David Shenk*, CIO Web Business, *October 1, 1999*

For attention mechanics to gain traction as a marketing discipline, it must be accompanied by sophisticated measures of communications performance.

In Silicon Valley, Steve Jobs, cofounder and CEO of Apple Computer, is admired for (among other traits) his ability to envelop bystanders in what's been called a "reality distortion field." When Steve gives a speech, even ordinarily skeptical industry analysts and observers have been known to lose their capacity for critical reasoning. Giant competitive threats from Microsoft or Japan or the diminishing pool of Apple-loyalist software developers become insignificant matters (or are simply forgotten) inside the reality distortion field.

Most marketers today design and test their campaigns inside a reality distortion field. They *assume* that consumers will notice and pay attention to their ads as long as they receive a prescribed number of eyeball exposures. However, if marketers could glimpse the real world outside, they would realize a critical fact: *Attention is not a given*. If we are serious about designing and implementing effective marketing communications programs, then attention must be measured.

# The Future: Measurement Shifts Downstream

In the future, measurement of campaign performance will have to shift downstream. Classic persuasion physics marketing focuses most measurement upstream—at the copy development stage. For example, TV commercials are frequently subjected to a series of gauntlets before they hit the airwaves: qualitative focus group commentary at the concept and storyboard stages, preliminary copy testing at the animatic stage, and theater-setting persuasion testing of the final version. All of these tests presume that we already have the consumer's rapt attention. But a funny thing tends to happen after this careful midwifery at the ad's birth: After ads are sent out into the marketplace, they receive little or no further measurement attention. There is no feedback loop, no measure of how well we did or how we could improve the next time. After the most painstaking of births, the children are sent into the jungle alone to fend for themselves.

Attention mechanics shifts the focus of campaign measurement downstream. Attention mechanics practitioners dote less intensively on the development of each creative message, instead demanding that far more ads be created and introduced into the marketplace. And once those ads start running, the focus of measurement is on their performance, live, in the real world.

Marketing consultant Alvin Achenbaum has observed that much of what passes for marketing research today is not even remotely scientific:

> As the most independent arbiters of truth, our Federal Court system has told us that marketing research, to be valid, must adhere to the scientific method . . . must adhere to rather stringent standards with respect to sample design and size, experimental design, questionnaire form, and interviewing and analytical discipline. Accordingly, it has deemed that findings from such widely used research methods as focus group sessions, mall intercept interviews, central location tests, and most copy research are inadmissible as evidence because they emanate from techniques which are considered patently unscientific and therefore invalid, untrue and misleading. . . . Hence, the courts are insisting on one standard—truth. Business is accepting a lower standard—falsity.[1]

# Efficiency Is Not Strategy

Attention mechanics will shift the measure of efficiency downstream. Today some brand marketers substitute efficiency for strategy during their communications planning process. (Efficiency measures are "cost-per" measures—cost per thousand audience, cost per click, cost per sale, and so on.) A typical packaged-goods approach is this: "Rank the efficiency of possible plan components and pick the most efficient ones to build the plan." It is surprising that this media planning method is not only tolerated but demanded by intelligent brand marketers. What if other fields worked this way?

Imagine an architect who has been awarded a skyscraper design project. If she operated as our "fictional" brand marketer does, then she would start by examining the efficiency of building materials: "Brick is less expensive than steel, but wood is less expensive than brick, and plastic and vinyl is less expensive than wood—we'll build the skyscraper with plastic and vinyl!" This is absurd, of course, but no less absurd than the approach of many marketing specialists today: "TV is more efficient than direct marketing or street theater, so we'll use TV!" Efficiency has a role to play, but only *after* the strategy is set. Efficiency must move downstream.

In an insightful essay, Michael Porter of the Harvard Business School answered the question, "Why do so many companies fail to have a strategy?"

> The pursuit of operational effectiveness [efficiency] is seductive because it is concrete and actionable. Over the past decade, managers have been under increasing pressure to deliver tangible, measurable performance improvements. Programs in operational effectiveness produce reassuring progress, although superior profitability may remain elusive. Business publications and consultants flood the market with information about what other companies are doing, reinforcing the best-practice mentality. Caught up in the race for operational effectiveness, many managers simply do not understand the need to have a strategy.[2]

Media buying clout and efficiency are levers that are becoming less important over time. In the future, the benefit of clout will be measured less by media pricing and more by the degree of access it allows to global media owners. Brand marketers with giant media budgets will want to engineer multimedia network brand sponsorships—and clout can open the door to such deals. The most forward-looking media leaders understand this. For example, my colleague, Bob Igiel, president of the Broadcast Division of The Media Edge, has been in the forefront of the movement to weave innovative cross-media programs with global media owners. For our AT&T client, Bob crafted a multiyear, multimedia football sponsorship that cuts across 15 different properties of The Walt Disney Company—including TV, the web, magazines, radio, out-of-home, and event elements, even an AT&T float in the Rose Bowl Parade! This is the benefit of clout—not the ability to grind out the lowest CPMs, but the ability to leverage size skillfully to create innovative, network brand sponsorships.

Considerations of effectiveness must come first, and considerations of efficiency must move downstream. Peter Drucker, the elder statesman of management theory, puts it this way: Strategy worries about doing the right things. Operations worries about doing things right. Doing the right things makes a company effective. Doing things right makes a company efficient. Both must be done well to maintain a competitive advantage, but effectiveness always trumps efficiency. There is no point to doing cheaply what should not be done at all.

## What to Measure

Attention mechanics will become a data-centric approach to marketing execution. Attention mechanics campaigns will increase the need for relevant data on ad performance—especially data on attention itself. Over time, the currency for ad buyers will shift from media ratings to actual attentive ad impressions.

### Can Attention Be Measured Directly?

Many observers in advertising research fields have long claimed that attention cannot be measured, at least directly. It's true that direct measurement of all the psychological and physiological dimensions of attention may never be feasible, significant progress has been made along these lines in recent years.

One intriguing study was recently undertaken in the Netherlands.[3] Researchers there wanted to measure the attention given to print ads. They used eye-tracking equipment to determine the effect of repeated exposures to ads. The researchers carefully recorded *saccades* (quick jumps of the eye from location to location) and *fixations* (the pauses between saccades), to piece together the duration, position, and pattern of the subjects' attention scanpaths. One of their conclusions is that, by the third exposure to an ad, people pay 50% less attention than they did to the first exposure. Repetition reduces attention.

Another example comes from Capita Research Group in Blue Bell, Pennsylvania. Capita Research has patented a system for measuring another indication of attention: brainwave activity. The system, called the Engagement Testing System™, uses electroencephalogram (EEG) technology to produce an Engagement Index, an objective measurement of whether audiences are actually paying attention to visual and auditory stimuli. The system has been adapted from work originally conducted by NASA to measure the alertness of astronauts as they performed their cockpit tasks. Capita Research has started applying its new technology to measure the attention-grabbing power of online banner ads and TV commercials.

Attention mechanics will demand intensive stewardship, measurement, tracking, and monitoring. Its adherents will want to drive marketing from a database with a continuous feedback loop to allow for ongoing adjustment and improvement.

The neurological basis of attention is not completely understood and not easily measured directly. Biological definitions of attention refer to the sequence and extent of the brain's electrical and chemical activity. Science tells us that the brain has 10 quadrillion ($10^{15}$) neural connections. When a minimum threshold of neurons are firing at a certain rate—voilà!—that's attention.[4]

Since it's not feasible to keep everyone hooked up to brain-scanning equipment all the time, marketing scientists will have to make do with reasonable surrogate measures, the footprints of attention.

A step in the right direction is to measure (or to estimate) "eyes on" or "ears near" during media exposures. As the growth in data (based on passive meter research, in-room spy experiments, and camera studies) supports these estimates, media buyers will want to optimize their media buys accordingly.

Higher up the ladder, marketers will evaluate the attention-getting effectiveness of their communications based on degree of involvement and interaction by consumers. Did they click through (i.e., bypass) the ad? How much time did they spend with the message? Did they follow referrals to other messages in the campaign? Did they raise their hands to request more information? Did they sign up? Did they register? Did they *convert?* Did they *buy!?*

Going forward, marketers will need to collect a *chain* of measures to gauge the impact of their communications efforts. For example, Ward Hanson, Stanford Business School professor and director of the Stanford Internet Marketing Project, has conceptualized an intriguing approach to online media measurement, which he calls *web chains.* A web chain describes all possible sequences of events that may occur as a result of online media exposure. Hanson has developed measurement metrics at each branch in the chain. The following is just a partial list of the metrics Hanson has conceptualized. A web chain begins when a prospect views a link to the brand web site, as shown in the accompanying table.

Ironically, the rise of the web as a new communications medium will give marketers a greater ability to determine the effectiveness of *non*web media. If brand ads in traditional media (TV, radio, magazines, newspapers, out-of-home) refer consumers to specific places on the brand's web site, then each traditional ad can be measured by the amount of activity it stimulates at the web site. Further, activity could be measured in terms of *head count* (traffic at the page) or *action* (inquiries, qualified inquiries, and sales). From these figures, approximate return on investment could be calculated for every ad in a campaign, whether online or offline.

Finally, marketers will increasingly measure the combined effects of all communications plan elements through awareness-tracking research.

### Web Chain of Events, Beginning with Viewers Who Are Exposed to a Paid Link

| Level | Action | Term | Key Measurement |
|-------|--------|------|-----------------|
| One | Don't notice | Nonviewers | No notice rate (NNR) |
| One | Notice but don't click | Viewers who received ad impact | 1-CTR-NNR |
| One | Notice and click | Prospects | Click-through rate (CTR) Clicks/views |
| Two | View site, don't buy | Nonconverted prospects | Nonconversion rate (1-CR) |
| Two | View site, buy later | Delayed buyers | Delayed buying rate 1-OIB |
| Three | View site, buy online now | Converted prospects (CP) | Conversion rate (CR) buyers/clicks |
| Four | Repeat customer, view site, buy online now | Loyal customer (LC) | Loyalty rate (LR) LC/CP |

*Source:* Adapted from *Internet Marketing* by Ward Hanson. Cincinnati: South-Western College Publishing, 2000.

The entire marketing communications program will be the unit of analysis, not just a single ad. Marketers will infer attention by measuring awareness of messages and, more important, awareness of brand propositions that the messages are designed to communicate. Multiple measures will be required to gauge the footprints of attention.

Online media planning and buying, as practiced today, provide a glimpse of what multimedia campaign management might be like in the future. In our firm, online media specialists spend far less time developing the media plan and far more time analyzing and managing online banner ad performance in real time—searching for signs of click-through fatigue and swapping in new ads to boost performance. The measurement has moved downstream.

This is exactly the reverse of traditional offline media buying and stewardship. The traditional process concentrates its effort up front, during the planning stage. Once the plan has been developed, the goal is to implement it as scheduled, with no changes. Attention mechanics

**Measuring the footprints of attention.**

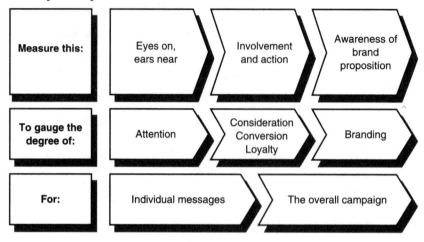

| Measure this: | Eyes on, ears near | Involvement and action | Awareness of brand proposition |
| To gauge the degree of: | Attention | Consideration Conversion Loyalty | Branding |
| For: | Individual messages | The overall campaign | |

expects changes. Attention mechanics is not a destination but a process for ongoing campaign improvement.

# On to Permission Marketing?

Although attention is a critical prelude to any marketing task, the final goal is not attention, but loyal sales. If attention and loyalty are the two ends of a balance, then marketing strategists must place equal weight on both ends to achieve success.

Over time, marketers have become fixated on loyalty. As a result, the loyalty end of the balance has become overweighted, and the balance is at risk for toppling over. Attention mechanics aims to restore the rightful balance between these two ends—because both are necessary. One alone will not succeed.

This book brings new thinking to the attention end of the balance. But there is new thinking at the other end as well. Of particular interest is *permission marketing*—an approach conceived by Seth Godin, vice president in charge of direct marketing at Yahoo![5]

Balancing marketing communications goals.

**Attention → Consideration → Purchase → Loyalty**

Permission marketing is based on the intriguing idea that the best way to gain loyalty is by gaining permission first: permission to send a marketing message, permission to turn a monologue into a dialogue, permission to engage in an evolving, learning relationship with the customer. Permission marketing shuns interruptive messages in favor of messages that consumers have given their permission to receive.

> Instead of annoying potential customers by interrupting their most coveted commodity, time, [permission marketing reaches] out only to those individuals who have signaled an interest in learning more about a product. . . . Permission Marketing enables companies to develop long-term relationships with customers, create trust, build brand awareness—and greatly improve the chances of making a sale.[6]

To gain permission, marketers must offer to trade something of value for the consumer's attention—some information, some service, or some entertainment.

American Airlines employs permission marketing when it sends weekly e-mails to consumers who have agreed to receive them. The e-mails alert consumers to low fares on undersold flights. Godin says that both the airline and its customers are delighted by the program: It doesn't cost the airline anything, and the people receiving the messages have the opportunity for discounted fares.

Web music marketer CDNow offers another example. CDNow uses permission marketing by sending e-mails to past customers informing them of new releases that might interest them. According to Godin, 40% of CDNow's sales directly result from this permission-based program.

But even Godin concedes that permission marketing is not always enough by itself.[7] By definition, consumers have to pay attention and signal their permission before permission marketing can take hold.

Attention mechanics provides the large footprint that permission marketing needs. Attention mechanics sweeps a wide path through the marketing landscape, scooping up hand-raisers and funneling them inside the "permission-to-message" recycling system.

Permission marketing is an attractive companion to attention mechanics. Attention mechanics and permission marketing are at opposite ends of the same marketing equation. Attention is a critical prelude to any marketing task. Persuasion, sales, and loyalty may be the ultimate aims of all marketing efforts, but none can be achieved without the consumer's attention.

May I have your attention please?

# 17

# Conclusion

The currency of the New Economy won't be money, but attention.
*Michael H. Goldhaber, "Attention Shoppers,"* Wired,
*December 1997*

Attention is a precious resource. Marketers and the media must no longer squander it, abuse it, or worst of all, take it for granted. Turning up the volume is no longer an acceptable response. If we do not change from our present course, we risk continued, and possibly accelerated, degradation in our communications effectiveness.

Attention mechanics offers an alternative path. Attention mechanics can help marketers steer a course from the old world we're leaving, where we expected ads to do things to people, to the new world we're now entering, in which we increasingly expect people to do things with ads.

Attention mechanics holds out the promise that marketers who balance the competing interests of persuasion and attention in their marketing programs will win. Attention mechanics also holds out hope to traditional advertising agencies willing to embrace its tenets. Those who possess a full menu of multidisciplinary communications capabilities (advertising, media, public relations, direct marketing, interactive marketing, sales promotion, and so on) and who acquire the skills to link and weave them together will win.

Attention mechanics offers an environmentally friendly code of conduct to marketers concerned about the future of the attention ecology.

We need attention mechanics now more than ever. People's capacity to pay attention is becoming overtaxed by the pace and complexity of modern life. The response of the media and marketing communities to this condition has been less than promising: Turn up the volume! Intrude! Interrupt! Scream! Assault! Offend! Imprison! And by all means, repeat, repeat, *repeat!!*

To be sure, these are ways to break through and get noticed. But at what cost? It is as if we have some earthmoving to do and are prepared to drop a nuclear bomb to do it. It gets the job done all right, but if everyone does it, there won't be many jobs left to do.

Marketers, their competitors, and consumers find themselves caught in a sort of cold-war standoff in which all sides refuse to budge until the other side moves first.

We have engineered a scenario of mutually assured destruction in the marketing sphere—the same strategy that kept the world on the brink of disaster for four decades following World War II. The application of force begets more force in an ever escalating spiral. Advertisers attack with TV commercials. Viewers defend with remote controls to *zap* (change the channels) and *zip* (fast-forward the VCR) commercials into oblivion. Telemarketers thrust with dinnertime phone solicitations. Consumers parry with call blocking and caller ID. E-mail spammers clog computer users' mailboxes. Users fight back with sophisticated filtering software. "Individuals need to realize there's a war going on between the market and consumers," observes author David Shenk. "It's a war for attention and time. The scarce resource is time."[1] Marketers must begin to recognize that hijacking consumers' attention through any means available is not a viable long-term business strategy.

The aim of attention mechanics is to prevent mutually assured destruction (MAD) and restore the power of marketing communications for the future.

James Young, cofounder of Young & Rubicam, once said, "If a man or a woman is at all fascinated by advertising it is probably because he or she is among the reconstructors of the world." The ambition of attention mechanics is to reconstruct the world of advertising.

As we begin the new millennium, marketers and ad agencies must learn how to restore the power of marketing communications. If we do not, then we must be content to travel down either of two paths: the path toward despair or the path toward total extinction. We can, and should, aim quite a bit higher than that.

# Notes

## Introduction

1 John Jones, "The Mismanagement of Advertising." *Harvard Business Review*, January–February 2000.

## Chapter 1 What's Wrong with Yesterday's Marketing?

1 Several of the examples in this chapter were first cited by David Shenk in his book *Data Smog: Surviving the Information Glut*. New York: HarperCollins, 1997.

2 Daniel Bell, *The Coming of the Post-Industrial Society*. New York: Basic Books, 1976.

3 James Gleick, *Faster: The Acceleration of Just About Everything*. New York: Pantheon Books, 1999.

4 Cited in *The Wall Street Journal*, January 11, 1999.

5 William Safire, Op-Ed essay, *The New York Times*, May 31, 1999, p. A19.

6 Cartoon signed BEK. *The New Yorker*, July 12, 1999.

7 David Ogilvy, *Ogilvy on Advertising*. New York: Crown, 1983, pp. 110–113.

8 All of these rules come from Charles L. Decker's book about P&G, *Winning with the P&G 99: 99 Principles and Practices of Procter & Gamble's Success*, New York: Pocket Books, 1998.

9 Decker, Charles L., *Winning with the P&G 99: 99 Principles and Practices of Procter & Gamble's Success*, New York: Pocket Books, 1998.

## Chapter 2 What Marketers Need Today

1 Cited in "One to a Customer," by Carol Hildebrand in *CIO Enterprise* magazine, October 15, 1999, pp. 62–66.

2 Doc Searls, interviewed by *The Industry Standard*. January 24, 2000.

3 Justin Hibbard, *Red Herring*, November 1999.

4 Evan R. Hirsh and Steven B. Wheeler. *Channel Champions. The Rise & Fall of Product-Based Differentiation*. San Francisco, CA: Jossey-Bass, 1999.

5 "ANA Examines E-tailing Dilemmas." *Advertising Age* magazine, October 18, 1999.

6 John Hagel III and Marc Singer. *Net Worth: Shaping Markets When Consumers Make the Rules*. Cambridge, MA: Harvard Business School Press, 1999.

## Chapter 3 Entering the Crowded Room

1 The study, *Efficient New Product Introduction*, was a collaboration among Ernst & Young LLP, the Grocery Manufacturers of America, and *Progressive Grocer* maga-

zine. And these are merely the competitors for space among the preexisting 35,000 items already carried by an average supermarket.

2    This idea comes from my colleague, Jay Dean.

3    ANA, *The Advertiser*, October 1997.

4    Caroline Cartellieri, Andrew J. Parsons, Varsha Rao, and Michael P. Zeisser, "The Real Impact of Internet Advertising," *The McKinsey Quarterly*, no. 3, 1997, pp. 44–62.

## Chapter 4    Interrupt Politely

1    Erwin Ephron, "Recency Planning: A New Media Approach." *Advertising Age* magazine, April 7, 1998.

2    *Media Matters*, January–February 2000.

3    Stephen Jay Gould, cited in *Natural History* magazine, June 1999.

## Chapter 6    Be Brief

1    Stephen Jay Gould, *Hen's Teeth and Horse's Toes*. New York: W. W. Norton.

## Chapter 7    Yell Occasionally

1    Kevin Keller, "The Brand Report Card," *Harvard Business Review*, January–February 2000.

2    "Applying Evolutionary Thinking to Brand Marketing," *Admap*, December 1998.

3    "What Really Happened at Coke." *Fortune* magazine, January 10, 2000.

4    Clayton Christensen, *The Innovator's Dilemma: When New Technologies Cause Great Firms to Fail: Taking the Path of Lowest Resistance*. Cambridge, MA: Harvard Business School Press, 1997.

5    Professor Alan Middleton, York University in Toronto, cited in "Putting the Fire Back into Brands," by Rance Crain, *Advertising Age* magazine, September 1994.

6    *Wall Street Journal*, October 21, 1999. Report by Svein L. Hwang, "Shock Overload Leads CNET to Redo Its Ads."

## Chapter 8    Whisper

1    Terry Lay, president, Lee Jeans, cited in "Great Ad! What's It For?" by Ellen Neuborne, *Business Week*, July 20, 1998.

2    Amir Malin, Artisan Entertainment, cited in *Fortune*, August 16, 1999.

3    Phil Guarascio, cited in "GM Gets a Running Start on Olympics Ads," *The Wall Street Journal*, June 18, 1999.

## Chapter 9    Be Different

1    *Coke Annual Report*, February 16, 1995.

## Chapter 10 Touch

1   Malcolm Gladwell, "Annals of Retail. Clicks & Mortar. Don't Believe the Internet Type: The Real E-commerce Revolution Happened Off-line," *The New Yorker*, December 6, 1999.
2   Michael Schrage, "Honest, I Am Not a Boor," *Fortune* magazine, November 8, 1999.
3   Megan Santosus, "But Wait, There's More," *CIO Enterprise* magazine, October 15, 1999.
4   Allan Falvey, "What's Next for Brands?" *BrandMarketing* magazine, September 1998.
5   Hilary Stout, "Ad Budget: Zero. Buzz: Deafening," *The Wall Street Journal*, December 29, 1999.

## Chapter 11 Tell a Story

1   Kevin Roberts, "Brand Identity 2000: Redefining the World," *Advertising Age* magazine, November 29, 1999.

## Chapter 12 Mingle

1   Peter Drucker, "Management's New Paradigms," *Forbes*, October 5, 1998.

## Chapter 13 Network

1   Alvin Achenbaum, "The Mismanagement of Brand Equity," ARF Fifth Annual Advertising and Promotion Workshop, February 1, 1992.
2   Leslie Heilbrunn, "Mind Control? (Not Yet)," *Brill's Content*, January 2000, pp. 105–110.
3   Rachel Weissman, "Convergence: The Message for Marketers," *American Demographics*, July 1999. Cited in an article by Elda Vale on the ZD Insider web site, December 8, 1999.
4   Charles Frenette, cited in "Coca-Cola Tells Shops: Capture Magic Moment," by Louise Kramer, *Advertising Age* magazine, October 25, 1999.
5   Evan Hirsch and Steven Wheeler, *Channel Champions*. San Francisco: Jossey-Bass, 1999.
6   Peter Rip, "Behavioral Targeting," an article on the Infoseek web site, October 25, 1999.
7   Seth Godin, "Build Permission with Spiral Customer Focus," *iMarketing News* magazine, July 23, 1999, p. 3.

## Chapter 14 Building a Networked Communications Plan

1   Michael McCarthy, "Viewers Sent to the Net for Endings of Nike Ads," *USA Today*, January 12, 2000.
2   Kevin Roberts, "Brand Identity 2000: Redefining the World," *Advertising Age* magazine, November 29, 1999.
3   Phil Guarascio, cited in "Sharp Curves Ahead for Car Marketers," by Jeff Green, BrandWeek magazine, January 3, 2000.

4 Roundtable discussion cited in *The Advertiser, Consumer Magazines*, October 25, 1999.

## Chapter 15  The Tools of Attention Mechanics

1 Alvin Achenbaum, "The Mismanagement of Brand Equity," ARF Fifth Annual Advertising and Promotion Workshop, February 1, 1992.
2 Michael Porter, "What Is Strategy?" *Harvard Business Review*, November 1996.
3 Rik Pieters, Edward Rosbergen, and Michel Wedel, "Visual Attention to Repeated Print Advertising: A Test of Scanpath Theory," *Journal of Marketing Research*, vol. XXXXVI, November 1999, pp. 424–438.
4 "When a number of nerve cells oscillate in synchrony at forty hertz—forty times a second—this *is* attention." Tors Norretranders, *The User Illusion. Cutting Consciousness Down to Size.* New York: Viking Penguin, 1998, p. 204.
5 Seth Godin, *Permission Marketing: Turning Strangers into Friends, and Friends into Customers.* New York: Simon & Schuster, 1999.
6 Seth Godin, in *Brand Marketing*, September 1999.
7 Seth Godin, "Build Permission with Spiral Customer Focus," *Imarketing News*, July 23, 1999.

# Acknowledgments

A number of friends and colleagues have influenced my thinking about attention.

First and foremost, Michael H. Goldhaber is, in my view, the high priest of attention. He has thought more deeply about the topic than anyone I know. Goldhaber has written and spoken extensively about the implications of "the attention economy" for many magazines, web sites, and conferences throughout the world. He is currently writing a book on the attention economy. Formerly a theoretical physicist, a Fellow of the Institute for Policy Studies in Washington, D.C., and editor of *Post-Industrial Issues*, Goldhaber is currently head of his own think tank, The Center for Technology and Democracy, and a visiting scholar at UC Berkeley's institute for the Study of Social Change.

Another stellar thinker on this subject is David Shenk. If there were a college course devoted to attention, Shenk's *Data Smog* would be a seminal text. (See Shenk, David. *Data Smog: Surviving the Information Glut*. New York: HarperCollins Publishers, 1997.)

Seth Godin's book, *Permission Marketing*, offers shrewd insights into the role of marketing communications *after* getting attention. Seth Godin is in charge of direct marketing for Yahoo! *Attention Mechanics* is a logical prelude for *Permission Marketing*. (See Godin, Seth. *Permission Marketing: Turning Strangers into Friends, and Friends into Customers*. New York: Simon & Schuster, 1999.)

I am grateful to Ed Papazian for reading an early draft of this book and offering numerous suggestions on how to improve it. Ed is the founder of Media Dynamics, Inc., and one of the country's most insightful media thinkers.

Two of my colleagues, Jay Dean and Austin McGhie, shaped my thinking most of all—not because I always agree with them, but because, as often as not, I don't. Still, few others think so deeply about these sorts of issues as this duo. And who knows? They might be right!

Also, I wish to thank my editors, Andrew Jaffe of *Adweek* and Ruth Mills of John Wiley & Sons, for guiding me and helping me make this a better book.

The following books also influenced my thinking in fundamental ways:

Pinker, Steven, *How the Mind Works*. New York: W. W. Norton & Company, Inc., 1997.

Christensen, Clayton, *The Innovator's Dilemma: When New Technologies Cause Great Firms to Fail: Taking the Path of Lowest Resistance*. Cambridge, MA: Harvard Business School Press, 1997.

I wish to thank my colleague, Mary Bond, for assistance and advice throughout the duration of this project. Thanks, Mary!

Finally, I wish to thank my wife, Miranda, for wise counsel and generous assistance throughout this project.

# Index